Penguin Handbooks
Budget Gourmet

Geraldene Holt trained as a potter and later qualified as a
teacher. She is married to the noted educationist Maurice Holt,
and she lives with her family in a sixteenth-century thatched
farmhouse in Devon.

Geraldene Holt's first book, *Cake Stall* (Penguin, 1983) was
written as a result of running a market stall in Tiverton selling
cakes, biscuits, cookies and scones using recipes that were
tried and tested during twenty years of family cooking and
entertaining. Her second book was *Travelling Food*, a guide to
picnics, packed lunches and away-day food, and as a result of
her frequent radio appearances she followed this with the
Devon Air Cookbook. Through her monthly food pages for
Homes and Gardens, her food columns for two West Country
newspapers and her regular contributions to television and
radio in the south-west, Geraldene Holt has become a well-
known and influential writer.

D1388804

Geraldene Holt

Budget Gourmet

Penguin Books

Penguin Books Ltd, Harmondsworth, Middlesex, England
Viking Penguin Inc., 40 West 23rd Street, New York, New York 10010, U.S.A.
Penguin Books Australia Ltd, Ringwood, Victoria, Australia
Penguin Books Canada Ltd, 2801 John Street, Markham, Ontario, Canada L3R 1B4
Penguin Books (N.Z.) Ltd, 182–190 Wairau Road, Auckland 10, New Zealand

First published by Hodder and Stoughton Ltd 1984
Published in Penguin Books 1985

Printed in Great Britain by
Richard Clay (The Chaucer Press) Ltd,
Bungay, Suffolk

Offset from Hodder and Stoughton edition

For Maurice, with love

ACKNOWLEDGMENTS

Recalling the extent of one's debt to others can be a hazardous, if not impossible, task for an author. So many people are eligible yet so few are recorded. I should, however, like to thank all my family, friends and fellow food enthusiasts who over many years have encouraged and influenced my cooking and attitude to eating.

I am also grateful to Morag Robinson who, once again, edited my work sensitively and with enthusiasm; my thanks also to Stephanie Darnill who tidied the script with such painstaking attention to detail.

My thanks are due to the writers and publishers, acknowledged in full overleaf, who have given permission for their recipes to be quoted.

Finally I am indebted to my husband, a true devotee of economy gastronomy and an unflagging seeker of edible bargains.

The author and publishers would like to thank the following for their kind permission to reproduce their recipes: Mr John Arlott for his Welsh Rarebit recipe from *Paxton and Whitfield Cheese Club Gourmet Guide to Cheese*; Nelson and Sons for Hummus Bi Tahina from *A Book of Middle Eastern Cookery* by Claudia Roden; Broomfield Publications for Mill Wheel Herb Loaf from *Cooking with Wholewheat Flour* by Doreen Chetwood; Marcella Hazan for her recipes for Pesto Sauce and Potato Gnocchi from *The Classic Italian Cookbook*; Jill Norman and Hobhouse Ltd for Potato Daube from *Simple French Food* by Richard Olney; Collins Publishers for Red Cabbage with Apple and Onion from *The Times Cookery Book* by Katie Stewart; J. M. Dent and Sons Ltd for Chicken cooked in Coconut Milk from *The Constance Spry Cookery Book* by C. Spry and R. Hume and for Poached Eggs in Wine Sauce from *The Tuscan Cookbook* by Wilma Pezzini; David Higham Associates Ltd for Marinade for Game from *French Provincial Cooking* by Elizabeth David; Macdonald and Co Ltd for Pigeon Pie from *Food in England* by Dorothy Hartley; Granada Publishing Ltd for Poached Pheasant with Celery Sauce from *Food for Pleasure* by Ruth Lowinsky; Macmillan, London and Basingstoke for Russian Salad from *The Russian Cookbook* by Nina Nicolaieff and Nancy Phelan; Faber and Faber Publishers for Cheese and Caraway Triangles from *The House of Viennese Cookery* by Trude Johnston and reprinted by permission of Penguin Books Ltd Merluza en Salsa Verda by Alan Davidson from Alan Davidson's *North Atlantic Seafood* (Penguin Handbook, 1979) p. 281, copyright © Alan Davidson, 1979, and Chocolate Chinchilla by Elizabeth David from Elizabeth David's *Spices, Salts and Aromatics in the English Kitchen* (Penguin Handbook, revised edition, 1975) pp. 223–4, copyright © Elizabeth David, 1970.

CONTENTS

INTRODUCTION

This book takes a fresh look at budget cooking. My approach differs from those who advocate that the cheapest is always the best. Concentrating solely on how to satisfy the appetite at minimum expense has more of the *budget gourmand* about it than the *budget gourmet*.

Too easily, eating can become a series of dismal meals revolving around minced beef, left-overs and packet soup which, above all, are intended to 'fill you up'. This lack of quality in eating can deaden one's awareness of food (always a dangerous thing) and deny one the pleasures of the table, the physical benefit and sense of total well-being to be gained from eating well. The notion of 'best', where eating is concerned, is usually more complicated than some writers would have us believe.

During the last ten years we have seen deep and permanent changes in our society which, in some ways, have altered our view of food. We are aware that we live in a multi-cultural society in a world of shrinking physical resources where nations are interdependent. The effects on our cultural thinking have varied from the growth of vegetarianism through the wholefood movement, to Nouvelle Cuisine with its welcome attention to process and flavour. Such changes in gastronomy can affect everyone's attitude to food, I maintain, for the better, leading to greater diversity and better use of ingredients.

Sadly, much that is written about budget eating is so joyless, the sheer sensual pleasure in eating seems to have been squeezed out of it in some depressingly puritan zeal. My approach is more optimistic, having realised some years ago, that my family and I were eating rather better than friends who were spending up to twice as much on food.

By eating better I mean eating delicious and varied food that doesn't take all day in the kitchen to prepare and yet is still exciting to cook and to consume. I suggest there exists only good cooking and non-good cooking and some of that is downright bad cooking. Surely good cooking, which implies a respect for food, will encompass 'budget cooking' in its very nature.

Meals should not be considered as entirely separate from each other, since each adds to a pattern, based on the seasons, different cultural backgrounds and a discrimination for fine food. In this way one works out a coherent style and philosophy of eating which gives one a sense of continuity against which new ideas can be tested. For me, eating is like a never-ending and interesting tapestry, hand-woven, with care, from the finest fibres to give subtle textures and shades of colour, embroidered in places with scintillating and exotic threads.

One of the least helpful approaches to budget eating is to set a limit of expenditure for each meal. Many institutions use this crude instrument of control and it is sometimes advised for domestic catering. But it leads to boring and repetitive eating. It is far better to stand further back and realise that on one day or for one week you will spend more and on others less. In this way certain foods such as wine or cream, coffee beans or butter, which are excised from many budget cooks' shopping lists, are welcomed into the cuisine for the essential part they play in good eating. There is no substitute for the best, only an inferior alternative. But the best can be used with discretion.

I was brought up in a home that was run on alternate periods of binge and bust. I know many who live the same way. But an inability to control food expenditure can lead to much heart-searching and worry. Most of us have times of financial insecurity during our lives—as students, when newly married, when self-employed or possibly, today, unemployed. Some are painful to recall. At such times food can occupy a major part of your thinking, but it can also contribute to your health and happiness. Even during periods of comparative hardship I have always managed to keep what a friend calls 'a good table'. But to be able to do so I have had to work out what I am doing and why. I very much hope that my approach will be of value to you.

A budget gourmet acts according to three precepts. The three principles are often seen as totally separate but in practice they interact so intimately that they are scarcely distinguishable.

The first principle is to *PLAN CAREFULLY*. This does not mean flicking through the pages of a vividly illustrated cookery book, waiting until a particular vision inspires one to cook. Naturally, certain considerations affect the initial thoughts about what food to plan. How many people do you intend to feed? Are any vegetarian? How much time do you have available for cooking? What did you eat yesterday? And what are you planning for tomorrow? What is the weather and the season? Is the meal balanced with regard to taste, texture, colour and nutrition? And there will be other constraints unique to your circumstances that will colour your thoughts. But, of course, it is simply unnecessarily expensive and possibly wasteful if such thinking is operating in a vacuum. Because to eat well is to eat with the best of food that is available.

This brings me to the second precept: *SHOP WISELY*. Your purchases are the fundamentals of your cooking. It is important to be able to judge between a good and a poor buy and to be flexible in those judgments. It is necessary, therefore, to have some standard of excellence.

Here is the opportunity to get out into the market place, garden, allotment and supermarket; to investigate what foods are in season, which are in the peak of condition, which are the best value, which are in surplus and are therefore at a bargain price. This is where the dynamic thinking and assessment involved in good cooking and eating come together. Seek out new sources of food. Be adventurous, try something new at least once a week and talk to shopkeepers and stall holders. You can never discuss food too much. One of the tragedies of supermarket shopping is the loss of helpful conversation between seller and shopper. Although you can usually find someone of whom you can ask a specific question, there is rarely anyone with whom to have a valuable exchange of information, or even just a friendly chat. This is one of the reasons that market stalls will never disappear and are, in fact, I am happy to say, flourishing.

All food purchasing is about choice: should we buy more

of a cheaper ingredient or less of a dearer one? Should we always buy 'mousetrap' cheese when a smaller portion of Stilton enables us to eat better for the same expenditure? Being a budget gourmet means appreciating the difference between 'la grande bouffe' of the English and the more restrained but prudent approach of the French. On the whole the higher the quality the less food you need because it is more satisfying.

Some choices are easy to make. Black pepper rather than white. Sea salt instead of rock salt. Both choices are made on the grounds of superior flavour. Once you have bought a mill for each, the difference in cost is small.

On the whole the recipes in this book specify butter rather than margarine. Although soft margarine can have a role in the kitchen, for dietary reasons or for fast baking—I found it helpful when I ran a cake stall to keep the family finances afloat—I mainly use butter in my cooking. Look out for the good-value unsalted butter on sale, now and again, from the EEC butter mountain and stock up if you can (butter freezes well—that's how the mountain doesn't melt away). Even in straitened times I have been able to continue to cook with butter once I realised that if you serve really fresh bread, as in France, there is no need for butter on it. I reckon most people spread about 10 grams (¼ ounce) of butter on each slice of bread and in a large family it adds up to quite an amount each week. I try to serve bread deliciously fresh, often warmed in the oven, and full of flavour. I bake smaller loaves that disappear at one meal and divide larger ones before freezing until needed. I no longer put butter on the table most days and no one seems to miss it—in fact we are probably all healthier.

Some of my recipes call for cream, double or single, but often in quite small amounts, just a tablespoon or two. I've found the best solution here is to buy frozen cream— Sainsbury's, Young's or Kerrygold, which, incidentally, is often cheaper than fresh cream and comes in convenient portions of 25 grams (about 2 tablespoons) each. It is simple to thaw one or more in a cup for adding to dishes, keeping the rest in the freezer until required.

14

Rarely have I lived where I am able to shop every day and so have come to depend upon a really well stocked larder and kitchen. Anyone interested in eating well will stock their cupboards with a wide range of spices, staples and storable food—half a dozen kinds of rice, anchovies, red peppers, black olives, a lump of Parmesan cheese in the fridge and herb butters in the freezer. These are the kind of ingredients which, used with discretion, unfailingly elevate the standard of one's cooking and enable new ideas and recipes to take shape. To me this is just part of good management, a kitchen quality that seems to count for rather less these days.

The third and most important principle of economy gastronomy is to learn how to *COOK WELL*, 'proper cooking' in Rosemary Hume's phrase, not cornflake cookery. This is the main theme and substance of this book, illustrated by a collection of varied recipes chosen from those I use at home and have used for many years. In today's often frantic search for novelty in food, where meals are seen as theatrical performances, there is rare encouragement to build up a repertoire of reliable and delicious recipes. Jean and Pierre Troisgros, in their famous restaurant in Roanne, offer a possible explanation, 'To do a good dish for a month is easy. To do it for twenty years, that is hard.'

While the gulf between the developed world as it moves into a post-industrial state and the rest of the world remains enormous, I maintain that good food is still cheap and remarkable value. People's memories about cheap food in the past perhaps account for the insistence on frugality in the housekeeping while paying ridiculous prices in restaurants whose often indifferent meals we regard as a 'treat'. We seem to have a puritanism about spending on food at home and misunderstand the true character of economy. In 1822 William Cobbett wrote in the introduction to his *Cottage Economy*:

The word Economy, like a great many others has, in its application, been very much abused. It is generally used as if it meant parsimony, stinginess, or niggardliness; and, at best, merely refraining from spending money. Hence misers and close-fisted men disguise their propensity and conduct under the name of

15

economy; whereas the most liberal disposition, a disposition precisely the contrary of the miser, is perfectly consistent with economy. Economy means management, and nothing more; it is generally applied to the affairs of a house and family, which affairs are an object of the greatest importance, whether relating to individuals or to a nation.

In making my choice of recipes, most of which I have devised, I have endeavoured to select not only good food but also those which cover a range of cooking processes, some of which are linked, and which, once mastered, equip one with a skill from which adventurous cooks can develop new and exciting ideas of their own.

Becoming a budget gourmet involves learning how to utilise your knowledge, your skill and your time to the full. It means making good food a priority in your life while according the best of ingredients their true respect. It means being an opportunist cook: able to take advantage of a cheap pheasant, a garden glut of home-grown fruit, even a bargain sack of gleaming carrots or an armful of free parsley. Louis Pasteur said that discovery favours the prepared mind; this is as true for gastronomy as for science. The reward is a higher standard of cuisine replete with the pleasure, benefit and satisfaction of eating well.

Clyst William Barton, Devon
July 1983

SOUPS
AND FIRST COURSES

Soups and first courses play a vital part in budget gourmet eating. Not only does a bowl of aromatic soup or a small salad provide an overture to a meal, introducing one to the style of the repast; perhaps making a welcome contrast, or a foretaste, but always a complement to the food to come. But, in the centuries-old tradition of cost-conscious eating, a first course assuages the appetite in a most satisfactory manner, enabling other courses to be less filling.

Many first courses arise naturally from proper management of the cuisine. The carcase from a chicken eaten a day or so earlier provides the basis for a soup for the meal, and any surplus will chill or freeze satisfactorily. There should never be any need to discard perfectly sound food; tales of egg yolks being poured away really grieve me. A bowl of cooked vegetables, or perhaps some boiled brown or white rice, not needed for the previous evening's meal make a basis for a cool, spiced salad to preface lunch.

If you find you are short of time for cooking, many of the dishes in this chapter can be prepared ahead. Others need be the only 'cooked' part of the meal, if you are happy to follow home-made soup with the best of 'instant' food; not some dehydrated substance tasting of monosodium glutamate, but a well-made loaf, farmhouse cheese and fruit in the peak of condition. There is a school of thinking which seems to indicate that if you fail to labour over a hot stove for at least two hours you haven't really cooked. I strongly disagree. It may be necessary to attend to a hot stove for only two minutes to produce food of high quality and distinction. The former represents the puritan view of cooking and eating—it must hurt to do you good. Certain dishes are regarded as 'wickedly' delicious or easy. It is such miserable nonsense. Good cooking and eating involves practice and discrimination. Of course, some food takes a long time to prepare but if the experience gained is to be valuable the process should be intensive rather than just extensive. Simply spending longer in the kitchen does not, alone, make you a good cook. Much of the best cooking is achieved quickly but with skill; the 'result of great experience and reflection', in the words of the Reverend Sydney Smith.

This brings me to the oft vexed question of stock; a pot or not and is a cube advisable? Of course, not all soups require stock. Many vegetable soups are simply a purée thinned with a béchamel sauce, milk, cream, yoghurt or its own cooking liquid. Naturally, if you have time, it is a counsel of perfection to have home-made stock in all its variety always to hand. Even a home-made stock resulting from simmering a carcase or bones with a few vegetables is valuable—especially if you are able to freeze any left over in cubes or plastic pots. On the other hand, if time is short or your circumstances do not allow for stockpiling, a quickly-made vegetable stock, produced while you prepare the rest of the meal, is often adequate. A dash of sherry or even a drop of soy sauce to this strained vegetable stock can make a brew that is altogether preferable to the commercial stock cube, which I find over-salty and artificial in flavour. It is, however, as with so many aspects of eating, a matter of personal choice.

Most soups are enhanced by the appropriate garnish, a sprinkling of chopped herbs, a swirl of cream, a few narrow strips of omelette or a neat julienne of vegetables. The right accompaniment can accentuate the delicious flavour of a home-made soup: crisp croûtons, triangles of hot potato pastry bubbling with cheese, or fingers of toast spread with a savoury butter. And, as always, a good loaf, be it home-made or from a reliable baker, can do a lot for almost all food and raise the standard of your eating.

Parsley Soup

Cooked parsley has a gentle fresh taste. Made for next to nothing with parsley from garden or window box, or even free from a fishmonger, this soup is a delight.

100 g	parsley, with stalks	3½ oz
1	small onion	1
	a sliver of garlic	
¾ litre	water or very light chicken or veal stock	1¼ pints
30 g	butter	1 oz
30 g	flour	1 oz
150 ml	creamy milk	¼ pint
1	small potato, peeled and diced	1
	salt, pepper	

Wash the parsley well and drain in a colander. Finely chop the onion and parsley. Cook together with the garlic, water or stock and some salt in an uncovered pan for 20–30 minutes or until the parsley is really tender.

Liquidise in a blender or processor, or push through a mouli-légumes on finest setting.

Melt the butter in the pan and stir in the flour for 1 minute. Add the parsley and liquor with the milk and cook, stirring, until thickened.

Add the finely diced potato and cook for 5–6 minutes or until tender. Check the seasoning and grind in a little pepper. Serve straight away or chilled.

Carrot and Orange Soup

Serves 6

The balance of the sweet carrot and the slightly sharp orange juice gives a harmony of flavours that makes an excellent soup.

500 g	carrots	1 lb
1	onion	1
60 g	butter	2 oz
600 ml	light chicken stock or water	1 pint
	salt	
2 teaspoons	sugar	2 teaspoons
300 ml	orange juice, unsweetened	½ pint
	pepper	
	rind of 1 orange	
4 tablespoons	double cream	4 tablespoons

Peel and dice the carrots and chop the onion. Melt the butter and soften the onion in it. Add the carrots and stir to coat with butter. Cover and cook gently for 5 minutes.

Add the stock, salt and sugar and cook, covered, for about 10 minutes or until the carrots are tender.

Purée the contents of the pan in a processor or blender, or push everything through a nylon sieve.

Reheat with the orange juice and check the flavour, adding more salt or sugar if necessary, and some pepper.

Just before serving, stir in the finely grated orange rind and the cream. Serve in hot bowls with croûtons or cheese straws.

Chiffonade of Lettuce

After talking about soups to my local W.I. I requested ideas for cheap soups. This simple but appetising soup using the outside leaves of a lettuce was one. Cooked lettuce resembles new peas in flavour.

1	whole lettuce or the outside leaves of 2	1
30 g	butter	1 oz
¾ litre	chicken stock or water	1¼ pints
30 g	rice	1 oz
	salt, pepper	

Wash the lettuce and discard the stalk and any tough parts. Shred it finely.

Melt the butter in a pan, add the lettuce and cook, stirring now and again, for about 10 minutes.

Add the stock and rice and cook, uncovered, for 15 minutes. Season to taste and serve.

Pondicherry Soup

Serves 6

Perhaps an unlikely combination of flavours: leek and, as the name implies, curry spices. But it works well and is one of my favourite soups.

500 g	young leeks	1 lb
30 g	butter	1 oz
2 teaspoons	curry paste	2 teaspoons
3 tablespoons	rice	3 tablespoons
900 ml	chicken or vegetable stock	1½ pints
150 ml	creamy milk	¼ pint
	salt, pepper	
3 tablespoons	thick cream	3 tablespoons

Trim the leeks and remove any tired outer leaves. Cut in half lengthwise and wash them really well under cold running water. Drain and slice them.

Melt the butter in a pan, add the leeks and stir. Cook, covered, over a low heat for 10–15 minutes until the leeks are tender.

Stir in the curry paste, rice and stock. Cover and cook for 10–15 minutes until the rice is tender. Sieve or blend the soup until smooth.

Reheat, season, and serve with a little cream spooned into each bowl.

Avgolémono

Serves 4–6

This famous Greek soup is always well received, being both delicious and nutritious, almost a complete meal for a slimmer.

900 ml	good, strong chicken broth, strained	1½ pints
60 g	long-grain rice	2 oz
2	eggs	2
	juice of 1 lemon	
	finely-chopped parsley	

The chicken broth can be made with the carcase of a chicken or poach a large leg of chicken with a selection of pot vegetables—onion, carrot, celery, etc.

Cook the rice in the strained broth until tender. In a bowl beat the eggs with the lemon juice. Gradually add 4–5 table-spoons of the boiling broth to the mixture, whisking continuously.

Pour the contents of the bowl into the broth, whisk well and allow to thicken over low heat, but on no account let the soup boil or it will curdle.

Serve straight away with a sprinkling of chopped parsley.

I always think of avgolémono as a summer soup but for colder days I add morsels of meat from the carcase and some slivers of the pot vegetables.

Brussels Sprouts Soup with Cheese Twists

Serves 4

I wouldn't have considered making soup with brussels sprouts, reckoning it would be too cabbage-like, until I heard Prue Leith recommending it. I tend to use loose or blown sprouts for it.

60 g	butter	2 oz
1	clove of garlic or onion	1
500 g	brussels sprouts	1 lb
2 tablespoons	flour	2 tablespoons
500 ml	chicken or turkey stock	¾ pint
	salt, pepper	
	grated nutmeg	
150 ml	creamy milk	¼ pint

Melt the butter in a pan and cook the chopped garlic or onion for 2–3 minutes. Trim the brussels sprouts and slice finely. Add to the butter, stir and cook gently until soft.

Stir in the flour and cook for 2 minutes then add the stock. Season with salt, pepper and nutmeg. Simmer the soup for 10–12 minutes.

Sieve or reduce to a purée in a blender or processor. Return to the saucepan and add the milk. Reheat, check the seasoning and serve very hot with cheese twists.

CHEESE TWISTS

120 g	puff or shortcrust pastry	4 oz
60 g	Parmesan or Cheddar cheese, grated	2 oz
	celery or caraway seeds	
	cayenne pepper	

Roll out the pastry, sprinkle with the cheese and seeds. Reroll a little and cut into finger strips. Twist each strip, dust with cayenne pepper and bake in a hot oven, 220°C, 425°F, Gas Mark 7, until crisp.

Potage Crécy

Serves 4–6

For most of the year carrots are a good buy. Here they make a butter-smooth soup.

350 g	carrots	12 oz
1	medium onion	1
60 g	butter	2 oz
600 ml	chicken or vegetable stock	1 pint
60 g	rice	2 oz
	salt and pepper	
300 ml	creamy milk	½ pint
2 tablespoons	chopped chervil or parsley	2 tablespoons

Scrub or scrape the carrots and slice thinly. Chop the onion. Melt the butter in a heavy based pan and slowly cook the carrots and onion, covered, for 15–20 minutes until soft.

Add the stock, rice and some salt and pepper. Cover and simmer for 15 minutes until the rice is cooked.

Sieve or blend the soup to a smooth purée. Return to the pan with the milk and reheat. Add the chervil or parsley and bring almost to the boil. Serve with hot wholemeal croûtons.

Fish and Corn Chowder

Serves 4

Considering we are an island we have surprisingly few traditional fish soups. This one I made up when my children were young.

150 g	haddock, cod, or coley, filleted	5 oz
300 ml	milk	½ pint
2	bay leaves	2
1	small onion	1
300 ml	stock or water	½ pint
250 g	sweetcorn, frozen or tinned	8 oz
1 tablespoon	cornflour	1 tablespoon
1	red pepper, chopped	1
	salt, pepper	
	chopped parsley	

Poach the fish in the milk with the bay leaves over gentle heat for 4–6 minutes. Meanwhile chop the onion finely and simmer in the stock or water for 5 minutes.

Drain the fish, reserving the milk. Flake the fish and add to the onion with the sweetcorn. Blend the cornflour with the strained milk and pour on to the soup with the chopped red pepper. Cook, stirring, until thickened. Season to taste with salt and pepper. Sprinkle in the chopped parsley and serve.

Cock-a-Leekie Soup

Serves 4–6

An excellent Scottish soup often seen on a Burns Supper menu. Its flavour is much improved by the inclusion of chicken giblets.

¼	fresh chicken, skinned	¼
	giblets from the chicken	
1 litre	water	1¾ pints
1	bay leaf	1
4	cloves	4
	a good sprig of thyme	
	salt	
2 tablespoons	rice	2 tablespoons
2	carrots, diced	2
1	turnip, diced	1
2	medium leeks, finely chopped	2
	pepper	

Put the chicken and giblets in a pan with the water, bay leaf, cloves, thyme and salt. Bring to the boil, remove any scum, then cover and cook gently until tender.

Throw in the rice, carrots, turnip and the white part of the leeks. Simmer for 10 minutes. Remove the chicken and giblets, discard the bones and chop the meat. Return to the soup with the green part of the leeks. Simmer for 7 minutes with the lid removed.

Check the seasoning, add some pepper to taste and serve.

Parsnip Soup with Anchovy Toast

Serves 4–6

Parsnip fanciers wouldn't agree with Eliza Acton's observation that parsnips have a 'peculiar flavour'. Here, their sweet earthy flavour is well accented by the salty anchovy toast.

½ kg	parsnips	1 lb
1	medium onion	1
1	stick celery	1
60 g	butter	2 oz
300 ml	chicken stock	½ pint
300 ml	creamy milk	½ pint
	salt, pepper	
	juice of ½ lemon	
2 tablespoons	chopped parsley	2 tablespoons

Peel and dice the parsnips and chop the onion and celery. Melt the butter and add the vegetables, stir and cover. Lower the heat and cook for 15–20 minutes or until the parsnips are completely tender.

Add the stock and sieve or blend to a smooth purée. Return to the saucepan with the milk and reheat.

Season to taste with salt and pepper and lemon juice. When really hot add the chopped parsley and serve with fingers of anchovy toast.

ANCHOVY TOAST

50 g	tin of anchovy fillets	1¾ oz
100 g	unsalted butter	3½ oz
	hot toast	

Drain the oil from the anchovies and rinse them briefly in tepid water. Drain and chop them finely. Beat the butter until soft and gradually work in the anchovies, or blend the ingredients together in a processor or blender until smooth.

Spread the anchovy butter on hot toast and cut into fingers.

Hazelnut and Celery Soup

Serves 4

A creamy satisfying soup for deep winter with a nutty taste and plenty of bite.

75 g	hazelnuts	2½ oz
45 g	butter	1½ oz
4–6	stalks celery, chopped	4–6
1	clove garlic, crushed	1
¾ litre	chicken stock	1¼ pints
	salt, pepper	
2 teaspoons	flour	2 teaspoons
150 ml	top of milk	¼ pint
	celery leaves, chopped	

If the hazelnuts are unskinned, roast them in a hot oven or under a grill until the brown skins are brittle and can be removed by rubbing the nuts in a cloth.

Melt the butter and sauté the nuts for 3–4 minutes until starting to change colour. Add the celery and garlic. Stir, lower heat and cook, covered, for 10 minutes.

Pour in the stock and add some salt and pepper. Simmer the soup for 10–15 minutes. Strain through a sieve reserving the liquor, add the flour to the nuts and celery and blend to a not-too-smooth purée in a processor or blender.

Return the purée and the reserved liquor to the pan and cook for 5–8 minutes until thickened. Add the top of milk and the chopped celery leaves, reheat and serve.

Terrine of Spring Vegetables   *Serves 8*

A food processor makes preparing this pretty and delicate terrine very simple indeed. An ideal dish to make ahead for a party.

	few spears of asparagus	
60 g	slim French beans	2 oz
bunch	new baby carrots	bunch
2	young slim courgettes	2
1 or 2	heads of broccoli	1 or 2
	a little sunflower oil	
250 g	breast of chicken, free of bone or skin, chilled	8 oz
1	egg white	1
300 ml	double cream	½ pint
¼ teaspoon	salt	¼ teaspoon
	white pepper	
⅛ teaspoon	grated nutmeg	⅛ teaspoon

Tomato sauce:

400 g	tinned tomatoes	14 oz
2	bay leaves	2

Trim the asparagus free of any tough ends. Leave the beans whole but remove the ends. Treat the carrots in the same way. Cut the courgettes into thin sticks and divide the broccoli into pieces.

Blanch or steam all the vegetables separately for 1–2 minutes. Cool each vegetable and season.

Line the base of a non-stick loaf tin of 750 ml (1¼ pts) capacity with non-stick silicon paper and rub lightly with sunflower oil. Chill in a refrigerator.

Cut the chicken into pieces, put into the processor and chop finely. Add the egg white and cream and process until smooth. Season with salt, pepper and grated nutmeg.

Spoon a thin layer of chicken into the tin. Arrange the asparagus spears on top, cut to fit, and cover with chicken mixture. Continue to arrange the vegetables separated by layers of chicken until the tin is full. Work as quickly as possible so that everything remains chilled.

Place a piece of non-stick paper, cut to fit, on top of the mixture and cook in a bain-marie in the centre of a moderate oven 180°C, 350°F, Gas Mark 4 for 50–60 minutes when the terrine should be firm all through. Allow to cool in the bain-marie then chill overnight.

Make the tomato sauce by sieving the tomatoes and their liquid into a pan. Add the bay leaves and simmer over moderate heat until reduced by half. Season with salt and pepper and chill until needed.

Loosen the terrine with a knife and turn out on to a flat plate. Cut into 8 slices and place each on a plate. Spoon a little tomato sauce around the terrine to heighten the colour and flavour.

Pasta and Mushrooms with Chervil

Serves 4

Chervil is far easier to grow than parsley and its slightly aniseed flavour enhances many vegetables and meats. Add the herb at the last moment for the greatest piquancy.

180 g	shell pasta	6 oz
	sunflower oil	
	large knob of butter	
	sliver of garlic	
180 g	button mushrooms	6 oz
	juice of ½ lemon	
	salt, pepper	
150 ml	soured cream	¼ pint
2–3 tablespoons	chopped fresh chervil	2–3 tablespoons

Cook the shell pasta in boiling salted water with a splash of sunflower oil until *al dente*. Drain and keep hot in a strainer over simmering water.

Melt the knob of butter in a pan and add the garlic impaled on a wooden skewer so that you can extract it later. Add the whole mushrooms and turn over in the butter. Pour in the lemon juice and add some salt and pepper. Cook the mushrooms quickly until just ready—they should still have some bite. Remove the garlic.

Stir in the cream and the chervil. Turn the pasta into a hot serving dish and spoon the mushrooms over.

Savoury Ham Cheesecake   *Serves 6 or more*

I have used the method of making a set cheesecake to a savoury end, and find it is popular as a first course or as part of a summer buffet.

Crumb base:

100 g	wholemeal and bran biscuits (Fox's are good)	3½ oz
60 g	unsalted butter	2 oz
	sunflower oil	

Cheesecake:

250 g	home-cooked or flavourful ham, diced	8 oz
1 tablespoon	powdered gelatine	1 tablespoon
150 ml	strong ham or chicken stock	¼ pint
250 g	cream or curd cheese	1 tablespoon
2 tablespoons	mayonnaise	2 tablespoons
1 tablespoon	tomato purée	1 tablespoon
2 tablespoons	dry sherry	2 tablespoons
	finely grated rind and juice of ½ orange	
	salt, pepper	
1	egg white	1
¼	cucumber	¼

Make the base first. Crush the biscuits and mix with the melted butter. Brush a 20 cm (8 in) wide round spring-form tin with sunflower oil, line the base with greaseproof paper and brush with oil.

Press the crumb mixture into the base. Smooth level with the back of a spoon and chill until firm.

Finely mince or chop the ham in a processor. Soften the gelatine in a little ham stock, then dissolve in the rest of the stock over low heat.

Cool and beat into the cheese with the mayonnaise, tomato purée, sherry and orange rind and juice. Fold in the ham and add salt and pepper.

Whisk the egg white until stiff and fold into the mixture. Spread on to the crumb base. Chill until set. This cheesecake improves if kept, covered, in the refrigerator for 1–2 days.

To serve, unmould carefully and place on a flat board or plate, leaving the greaseproof paper and base in place. Decorate with thinly sliced cucumber around the edge.

Celeriac with Smoked Mackerel Dressing
Serves 4

An uncommonly good salad, excellent as a first course.

500 g	celeriac	1 lb
1	large fillet smoked mackerel	1
	juice of 1 lemon	
150 ml	soured cream	5 fl oz
1 tablespoon	finely chopped chives	1 tablespoon
	salt, pepper	
	few leaves of chervil, to garnish	

Peel the celeriac and grate finely into a bowl.

Remove the skin and any bones from the fish and flake into a processor or blender. Whizz to a purée with the lemon juice and mix with the soured cream and chives. Season with salt and pepper.

Pour the dressing over the celeriac and toss until completely coated.

Serve on small plates, sprinkled with leaves of chervil.

Hummus Bi Tahina

Serves 4–6

Now that pitta bread is so widely available in grocers and supermarkets and it freezes well too, it is worth making its happy companion, Hummus. Serve this dish of puréed chick peas and tahina, from *A Book of Middle Eastern Food* by Claudia Roden, as an hors d'oeuvre or build an outdoor meal round it.

180 g	chick peas	6 oz
2–3	lemons	2–3
2	cloves garlic, crushed	2
	salt	
150 ml	tahina paste	¼ pint
1 tablespoon	olive oil	1 tablespoon
1 teaspoon	paprika	1 teaspoon
1 tablespoon	finely chopped parsley	1 tablespoon

Soak the chick peas in water overnight. Drain and simmer in water to cover for about 1 hour or until soft.

Strain through a colander and keep back a few for decoration. Turn the chick peas into a processor or blender with the juice of the lemons, the garlic, some salt and the tahina paste.

Whizz to a purée, adding a little water if necessary until the hummus is like mayonnaise.

Spoon into a serving dish. Mix the oil with the paprika and pour over the surface of the hummus. Arrange the reserved chick peas in a pattern on top and sprinkle with the chopped parsley. Serve with pitta bread warm from the oven.

Grapefruit with Prawns and Celery

Serves 4

From February to April grapefruit are usually a good buy. Halved and grilled with honey and a little sherry or rum they are excellent. Or, as here, cut in half, Van Dyke style, and filled with a mixture of prawns and celery tossed in mayonnaise spiked with a touch of curry paste. When prawns are too dear, replace with diced chicken or ham.

2	large grapefruit	2
120 g	peeled prawns	4 oz
2	sticks crisp celery	2
½ teaspoon	curry paste (Patak's Tikka)	½ teaspoon
4 tablespoons	mayonnaise	4 tablespoons

Halve the grapefruit and with a small serrated knife cut out the segments of flesh, free of skin or pith, into a bowl. Scrape the grapefruit shells clean and with a knife or scissors cut V-shapes from the rim to give a pretty Van Dyke edge. Chill the grapefruit shells until needed.

Add the prawns and chopped celery to the grapefruit flesh. Mix the curry paste with the mayonnaise and just before serving spoon over the grapefruit mixture. Divide between the grapefruit shells and serve.

Tagliatelle Verde with Ricotta and Walnuts

Serves 4–6

This is my returning-from-London dish. Armed with fresh pasta and ricotta it can be put together in under 10 minutes.

500 g	fresh tagliatelle (see p. 82)	1 lb
	salt	
	few drops sunflower oil	
45 g	butter	1½ oz
100 g	walnuts, halved or broken	3½ oz
350 g	ricotta cheese	12 oz
	milled pepper	

Cook the pasta in boiling salted water with the oil until *al dente*. Meanwhile heat a serving dish with a knob of butter in it.

Melt the rest of the butter and sauté the walnuts until golden and sweet smelling.

Drain the pasta in a colander, turn into the serving dish and toss in the butter. Spoon the ricotta cheese over the pasta and scatter with the hot walnuts. Mill plenty of salt and black pepper over and serve.

Cream of Tomato Soufflé

A pretty pink cold soufflé, excellent filled with shellfish, chicken or ham for a summer lunch, or try a salad of tuna fish, Jerusalem artichokes and black olives in the winter.

1 tablespoon	butter	1 tablespoon
1	onion, finely chopped	1
1	stick celery, chopped	1
¾ kg	ripe tomatoes, skinned and chopped	1½ lb
½ teaspoon	sugar	½ teaspoon
	salt, pepper	
1 wineglass	dry white wine	1 wineglass
1 tablespoon	powdered gelatine	1 tablespoon
150 ml	consommé or jellied beef stock	¼ pint
150 ml	whipping cream	¼ pint
1	egg white	1

Melt the butter in a pan and soften the onion and celery in it until golden and transparent. Add the tomatoes, sugar, salt, pepper and wine. Bring to the boil, then simmer gently for 30 minutes until thick.

Sieve the contents of the pan. Dissolve the gelatine in the consommé over gentle heat and stir into the tomato purée. Chill until just starting to set.

Whip the cream and whisk the egg white until stiff. Fold the cream and the egg white into the tomato mixture and incorporate properly with a balloon whisk.

Pour into a chilled 20 cms (8 ins) ring cake tin. Chill until set. Dip briefly in warm water and turn the soufflé out on to a flat serving dish and fill.

Mill Wheel Herb Loaf with Tapenade

Serves 4–8

The herb bread comes from Doreen Chetwood's *Cooking with Wholewheat Flour*; serve fresh from the oven with Provençal tapenade for a rustic meal full of earthy flavours.

1 mug	warm water	1 mug
1 teaspoon	honey or brown sugar	1 teaspoon
3 teaspoons	dried yeast	3 teaspoons
	or	
30 g	fresh yeast	1 oz
2½ mugs	wholewheat flour	2½ mugs
½ mug	porridge oats or wheat flakes	½ mug
1–2 teaspoons	salt	1–2 teaspoons
3 tablespoons	chopped mixed fresh herbs: parsley, chives, thyme, etc.	3 tablespoons
	or	
1 tablespoon	dried mixed herbs	1 tablespoon
1 tablespoon	sunflower oil	1 tablespoon

Pour the warm water into a mixing bowl and stir in the honey or sugar. Sprinkle in the dried yeast or crumble in the fresh yeast. Stir and leave in a warm place for 10 minutes to froth.

Add the wholewheat flour, porridge oats, salt, herbs and oil, and mix to a soft dough. Add more water if the mixture is too stiff.

Turn the dough on to a lightly oiled surface and knead for 2–3 minutes until smooth and elastic. Shape into a circle and place on a greased and floured baking sheet. Brush with oil and sprinkle oats or wheat flakes on top. Mark into 8 wedges with a sharp knife.

Cover with a plastic bag and leave in a warm place for about 30 minutes, until the dough is puffy and springs back when lightly pressed.

Remove the bag and bake the loaf in a very hot oven, 230°C, 450°F, Gas Mark 8, for about 30 minutes until firm and crusty and sounds hollow when tapped underneath. Move on to a wire tray to cool or into a cloth-lined basket for serving.

TAPENADE

This dark and aromatic sauce takes its name from one of its main ingredients—capers, or *tapeno* in Provençal.

120 g	black olives	4 oz
50 g	tin anchovy fillets	1¾ oz
4 tablespoons	capers	4 tablespoons
60 g	tuna fish	2 oz
1	lemon	1
about 100 ml	olive or sunflower oil	3–4 fl oz

Stone the olives (this is very easy if you freeze them overnight and then thaw) and put into the bowl of a processor or blender. Add the briefly rinsed anchovy fillets, capers, tuna fish and the juice of half the lemon.

Whizz to a purée. Now continue on slow speed, adding the oil through the lid. Check the taste and add more lemon juice if required. Spoon into a pottery bowl to serve.

Consommé Granita

If you find yourself with the remains of a bottle of good red wine left over, here is one of my favourite ways of using it. Serve in small glasses or dishes as a first course or between heavier courses to refresh the palate.

150 ml	drinkable red wine	¼ pint
150 ml	cold water	¼ pint
1	clove garlic, split	1
1	bouquet of fresh herbs including a bay leaf	1
411 g	tin Sainsbury's beef consommé or home-made	14½ oz
2–3 tablespoons	ruby port (optional)	2–3 tablespoons

Preferably in a glass saucepan (this prevents any reaction between acid and metal), simmer the wine with the water, garlic and the bouquet of herbs for 4–5 minutes.

Remove from heat and lift out the garlic and herbs. Stir in the consommé and port. Stand the saucepan in cold water and stir the liquid until cool.

When cool either freeze in the saucepan, covered, or pour into a lidded plastic box. After one hour stir in the mush from the outside of the pan and refreeze for another hour. As its name reveals, the granita should be grainy and only just frozen.

Serve in small glasses with teaspoons and accompanied by hot croissants.

FISH

For budget gourmets short of cooking time, fish is a great friend. It responds so well to quick yet gentle cooking but still leaves plenty of scope for inspiration. Usually the only difficulty is in getting hold of the stuff.

This is no problem if you fish yourself or live near a fresh fish shop plying its trade in a proper fashion; selling a good selection of produce that reflects the changing seasons. How sad that an island like ours, surrounded by fish-rich seas, has allowed what is, in truth, one of its staple foods to diminish in importance in its diet. A visit to Norway shows us what we are missing. Today in many parts of Britain the ubiquitous fish finger is the only fish that millions eat. And fresh mackerel and herrings are turned aside for imported prawns served in imported avocado pears in pursuit of 'smart food'.

This highly perishable food needs to be cooked the day it is bought or, if robust enough, frozen as soon as you get it home.

On the whole, apart from summer salmon we neglect cold fish dishes, such as mackerel cooked in tea or Japanese sashimi. These have the further advantage of being prepared when the fish is at its best, for eating a day or so later.

Choosing fish is not difficult if you remember that the best fish is fresh fish. It should look attractive and bright of eye. The flesh should still be fairly firm; reject any fish with an unpleasant smell. At the risk of upsetting the makers of refrigerated slabs, my favourite fishmonger tells me that he considers the old-fashioned marble slab far more hygienic. In my experience, I have had far less cause for complaint with fish bought from fishmongers still using them, but that may be sheer chance.

The best advice when buying fish is to find a good fish-monger and cosset him—they are a dying breed. There is, though, a chink of light in the gloom with the appearance of 'in-store' fresh fish stalls that are starting in some supermarkets. Having found your fish supplier, shop there frequently; fish is still an excellent buy and it makes you feel good. Your fishmonger will guide your purchases, enabling you to benefit from the best of the catch and help you to extend your knowledge of this underrated and precious food.

47

Halibut En Papillote
with Seville Orange

Serves 4

Orange goes well with white fish and this recipe is ideal for the start of the year when Seville oranges are around. It is always worth freezing some for later on. Try cooking other flat fish en papillote to conserve all their flavour.

½–¾ kg	halibut, filleted	1–1½ lb
	salt, pepper	
45 g	butter, melted	1½ oz
1	Seville orange	1
1	clove garlic, finely chopped	1
150 ml	single cream	¼ pint
	chopped parsley	

Divide the fish into four portions and season with a little salt and pepper. Brush with butter four pieces of greaseproof paper (or foil) large enough to wrap each piece of fish. Place the fish in the centre of each.

Cut 4 slices from the orange and place one on each piece of fish, then brush with butter. Fold up the paper or foil so that the join is on top and secure firmly, by folding, or resort to paper clips or staples as long as you can be sure of recovering them.

Place the paper or foil envelopes on a baking dish in a moderate oven, 180°C, 350°F, Gas Mark 4, for 12–15 minutes or until the fish is cooked.

Meanwhile squeeze the juice from the rest of the orange and add 1 tablespoon of finely grated zest.

Gently cook the garlic in the rest of the butter until golden. Add the orange juice and rind and cook for a minute or so. Lower the heat and add the cream.

To serve, open the envelope and slide the fish on to hot plates. Sprinkle with chopped parsley and spoon the sauce to one side of the fish.

Farm Trout Stuffed with Oatmeal and Herbs

Serves 2

While the number of fresh fish shops has fallen in recent years the number of trout farms has grown. Last year they produced 7,000 tonnes of trout, yet only seventeen per cent is bought for eating at home. Unlike most other fish, trout is becoming more easily available; here is a simple, yet good, way to cook them.

Stuffing:

4 tablespoons	medium oatmeal	4 tablespoons
2 tablespoons	hot water	2 tablespoons
2 tablespoons	chopped chives or spring onions	2 tablespoons
2 tablespoons	chopped parsley	2 tablespoons
1 tablespoon	chopped chervil if available	1 tablespoon
	salt, pepper	
2	fresh trout, medium or small	2
	a little butter	
2	lemon quarters	2

In a bowl mix the oatmeal, water, herbs and seasoning together until the stuffing binds.

Clean the fish and remove the heads if you wish. Spoon half the stuffing into each fish.

Butter two sheets of foil and wrap a fish in each.

Place in an oven dish and bake in a moderate oven, 180°C, 350°F, Gas Mark 4, for 20–30 minutes depending on size. The fish is cooked when the bone comes away cleanly from the flesh. Unwrap and serve the trout with lemon quarters.

Lemon Monkfish Kebabs

Serves 3–4

It is always worth snapping up monkfish and this is a most successful way of cooking it. Cod or haddock work almost as well.

½ kg	monkfish	1 lb
3 tablespoons	mild olive oil or sunflower oil	3 tablespoons
	finely grated rind and juice of 1 lemon	
1–2 tablespoons	chopped parsley	1–2 tablespoons
	salt, pepper	
120 g	button mushrooms (optional)	4 oz
	fat spring onions or small onions, quartered	

Trim any skin or loose tissue from the monkfish and cut into 4 cm (1½ in) chunks. In a shallow dish mix the oil with the lemon rind and juice, parsley, salt and pepper. Turn the fish in the marinade and chill, covered, for 1–2 hours.

Thread the fish on to 3 or 4 skewers, alternating the fish with mushrooms and onions. Brush with the rest of the marinade and grill under high heat for 10–15 minutes turning now and again.

Serve the kebabs resting on a dish of plain boiled rice or noodles.

Mackerel Cooked in Tea

Serves 4

Mackerel must be really fresh to be enjoyed, and catching your own is ideal. Avoid any that are soft bellied due to feeding in over-plentiful waters, which sometimes happens at the start of the season. A rich fish such as this is good served cold and this unusual recipe is surprisingly delicious.

4	mackerel	4
4	bay leaves	4
12	black peppercorns	12
	salt	
1 tablespoon	soft brown sugar	1 tablespoon
75 ml	cold, milk-less tea	3 fl oz
75 ml	white wine vinegar	3 fl oz

Behead and clean the fish and remove the backbone if you wish. Arrange in a single layer in an ovenproof dish with a bay leaf to each fish. Sprinkle with the peppercorns and salt.

Mix the sugar with the tea and vinegar and pour over the fish. Cover with foil and bake in a moderate oven, 180°C, 350°F, Gas Mark 4, for about 30 minutes until cooked.

Cool and then chill. The liquid will be lightly set and the fish will have a delicate flavour.

Jansonn's Temptation

Serves 4–6

A famous Swedish dish, introduced to us by a Swedish boy who came to stay one summer. Excellent served alone as a first course or as a vegetable course. For an even richer version use all cream.

600 g	waxy potatoes like Desirée, peeled	1¼ lb
	knob of butter	
2	medium onions, finely sliced	2
2×50 g	tins anchovy fillets	2×1¾ oz
150 ml	single cream	¼ pint
75 ml	top of milk	3 fl oz
	salt	

Cut the potatoes into matchsticks or grate coarsely. Drain the oil from the anchovies and reserve. Cut the wider fillets in two.

Butter a gratin dish. Make a layer of potato, season, but be sparing with the salt. Cover with a layer of onion. Arrange the anchovy fillets criss-cross on top. Complete with a layer of onion and then the rest of the potatoes. Season.

Pour over the oil from the anchovies and half the cream mixed with the top of milk. Dot with the rest of the butter.

Cook in a moderately hot oven, 200°C, 400°F, Gas Mark 6, for 35 minutes. Pour in the rest of the cream and cook for a further 10 minutes.

Seafood Pancakes

Pancakes or crêpes epitomise budget gourmet practice—the thinner the pancakes the more delicious and better value the result. This recipe is fine for pancakes with sweet or savoury fillings. As an alternative, try well-seasoned mixtures of vegetables, diced meat or fish, or spiced fruits, cream cheese and nuts.

Batter:

120 g	plain flour	4 oz
¼ teaspoon	salt	¼ teaspoon
250 ml	milk	8 fl oz
3	eggs	3
2 tablespoons	butter, melted	2 tablespoons

Filling:

350–500 g	mixed seafood—white fish, shelled prawns, scallops, mussels, etc.	12–16 oz
500 ml	water	¾ pint
small wine glass	white wine	small wine glass
1 slice	onion	1 slice
1	bay leaf	1
30 g	butter	1 oz
30 g	plain flour	1 oz
4 tablespoons	double cream	4 tablespoons
	chopped parsley or chervil	

Make the pancake batter ahead, if more convenient, adding the melted butter just before cooking. Sieve the flour and salt into a bowl, make a well in the centre and add almost all the milk and the eggs. Whisk lightly until the flour is incorporated but don't overbeat or the pancakes may be rubbery. Set aside for the batter to thicken as the starch expands.

Make the filling by poaching the white fish in the water, white wine, onion and a bay leaf. Flake the fish and strain the stock and reduce over high heat to 300 ml (½ pint). Poach the shell fish until cooked, lift out and add to the fish.

Melt the butter and, off-heat, add the flour and stir for a minute or so. Gradually whisk in the fish stock and cook, stirring, until thickened. Stir in the cream, then the seafood and keep hot.

Stir the melted butter into the batter and if too thick add the rest of the milk.

Heat a 18 cm (7 in) pancake or omelette pan and a hazelnut sized piece of butter. Run it over to grease the inside of the pan. With luck you won't have to butter the pan much again but repeat in this way if you do. The pan is at just the right heat when a small drop of batter sizzles at once.

Using a ladle or small cup, pour 2–3 tablespoons of batter into the pan, tilting the pan to run the mixture across the base. Cook until the top of the pancake is set. Toss or turn over with a knife, spatula or fish slice and cook the other side until golden. Turn on to a cloth on a wire rack and continue to cook the rest of the pancakes.

You should get at least a dozen pancakes from the mixture and with practice even more.

Take each pancake and place a spoonful of filling in the centre and roll up neatly. Place side by side in a hot buttered fireproof dish and cover with buttered paper. Reheat until sizzling in a moderate oven, 180°C, 350°F, Gas Mark 4. Sprinkle with parsley or chervil and serve.

Sprats Baked with Salt

Serves 4

Sprats must be one of the best value fish but are sadly underrated. This is my favourite way of cooking them: there is no surplus fat and the fish is seasoned as it cooks.

¾ kg	fresh sprats	1½ lb
3 heaped tablespoons	fine sea salt	3 heaped tablespoons
1	large lemon	1

Leave the sprats whole. Wash briefly in cold water, drain well and pat dry with kitchen paper.

Spread the salt in an even layer on a baking sheet.

Arrange the sprats in rows on the salt. Bake in a moderate oven, 180°C, 350°F, Gas Mark 4, for about 8 minutes or until the fish are cooked.

Use a fish slice to lift the fish, free of salt, on to a hot serving dish. Cut the lemon into wedges and arrange around the fish. Serve with crusty bread.

Moules Marinière

One of the best of all mussel recipes. Cook the mussels the same day that you buy them. Remember that each ½ litre or pint of mussels yields only 100 g or 3–4 oz edible mussel, so it is no bad thing to buy a few more than the recipe recommends to cover damaged ones.

2 litres	mussels	4 pints
150 ml	dry white wine	¼ pint
150 ml	water	¼ pint
	the white part of a leek, finely chopped	
	parsley stalks	
6	black peppercorns, crushed	6
	a little salt	
45 g	butter	1½ oz
3 tablespoons	chopped parsley	3 tablespoons

Clean the mussels by scrubbing them well under cold running water and pull away the 'beard' of threads from each one. Discard any mussels that will not close completely when tapped or any that are unnaturally heavy due to mud or sand. Drain the mussels in a colander.

In a wide pan, simmer the wine and water with the leek, parsley stalks, peppercorns and salt for 3 minutes. Gently add the mussels. Shake the pan and cover tightly with a lid or board. Raise the heat and allow to cook for 1 minute, shaking the pan, then remove from the heat. Leave, covered, for 5 minutes for the mussels to open in the steam.

Strain the mussels through a colander reserving the liquid, and reject any that have not opened. Turn the mussels into a hot tureen and cover with a cloth. Return the liquor to the pan, discarding the parsley stalks. Whisk in the butter, add the chopped parsley and pour over the mussels. Serve with hot crusty bread.

Japanese Sashimi

Serves 4

Just as in Ceviche or Séviche, in this recipe, which was given to me by a North Sea diver, raw fish is marinated in a highly acid mixture for twenty-four hours until the flesh has become opaque and appears to be cooked. Mackerel, for example, takes on an entirely different character. I highly recommend this dish for summer eating.

4	really fresh mackerel, whiting or sole	4
1	onion, thinly sliced	1
1	green or red pepper, seeded and sliced	1
	short piece fresh ginger, peeled and sliced	
3 or 4	lemons or limes, juice of	3 or 4
	white wine vinegar	
1	clove of garlic, crushed	1
1 tablespoon	white or brown sugar	1 tablespoon
1–2 teaspoons	soy sauce	1–2 teaspoons
4 tablespoons	sunflower oil	4 tablespoons

Wash the fish and fillet and skin the flesh. Cut very thinly into flakes and place the fish in a deep dish.

Arrange the sliced onion, pepper and ginger on top. Squeeze the juice from the lemons or limes into a measuring jug. Add an equal amount of wine vinegar, the garlic, sugar and soy sauce. Mix well and pour over the fish. Cover the dish with plastic film and chill in the refrigerator for twenty-four hours.

Strain 4 tablespoons of the liquor into a bowl and whisk in the oil to make a dressing. Arrange the fish on a bed of lettuce and pour the dressing over. Serve with bread or rice.

Smoked Fish Boulettes
with Sauce Chivry

Serves 3–4

Much nicer than fish cakes, these fish balls take no longer to make. Try them also with a fresh tomato sauce in the summer.

500 g	smoked haddock or whiting, skinned and filleted	1 lb
250 g	fresh white breadcrumbs	8 oz
1 tablespoon	chopped parsley	1 tablespoon
1	egg white	1
	a little butter	
1 wineglass	white wine	1 wineglass
1 wineglass	water	1 wineglass

Sauce Chivry:

150 ml (approx)	milk	¼ pint (approx)
20 g	butter	¾ oz
20 g	flour	¾ oz
1 tablespoon	cooked spinach, fresh or frozen, sieved	1 tablespoon
1 tablespoon	fresh mixed chives, chervil, tarragon, finely chopped	1 tablespoon
	salt, pepper	

Mince or process the fish until smooth. Put the breadcrumbs in a nylon sieve and run under cold water until really wet. Squeeze out as much moisture as possible and mix in with the fish, adding the parsley and, gradually, the egg white. The mixture should be fairly stiff.

Take dessertspoonfuls and shape into balls. Arrange in a buttered oven dish and pour over the wine and water. Cover with foil or a buttered paper and poach over moderate heat for 10–15 minutes or bake in a moderate oven, 180°C, 350°F, Gas Mark 4, for 15–20 minutes.

Remove the boulettes to a serving dish and keep hot. Strain the liquid into a jug and make up to 300 ml (½ pint) with milk.

To make the sauce, melt the butter in a pan, stir in the flour and then gradually whisk in the liquid and cook until thickened. Add the spinach and herbs and cook for a few minutes. Season to taste, spoon over the fish boulettes and serve.

Merluza En Salsa Verde
(Hake in a Green Sauce)   *Serves 6*

One of our favourite fish dishes from Spain. Use plenty of fresh parsley. From *North Atlantic Seafood* by Alan Davidson.

6	thick steaks of hake	6
1	lemon	1
	olive oil	
4	cloves garlic, peeled	4
3–4	medium sized potatoes, thinly sliced	3–4
1 tablespoon	flour	1 tablespoon
½ cup	cold water	½ cup
	salt	
1	bay leaf	1
4 tablespoons	chopped parsley	4 tablespoons

Wash the fish and pat dry on kitchen paper. Squeeze the juice of the lemon over them.

In an earthenware casserole or wide enamelled frying pan, heat enough oil for frying the potatoes. First brown the garlic in the oil and then remove to a mortar. Now lightly fry the potatoes. Off the heat add the flour blended with the water and continue to cook until the potatoes are soft.

Season the hake steaks with salt and add them to the pan with the bay leaf. Pound the garlic with the parsley and add to the pan. Continue to cook, shaking the pan occasionally for 20–30 minutes until the fish is tender.

Sprinkle with a little more chopped parsley at the last moment, and serve from the cooking dish.

Crab Creole

A few years ago an enterprising fisherman from Brixham started door-to-door deliveries in our East Devon village with his freshly caught produce. We feasted on crab nearly every week that summer—they were so good and wonderful value. Working through many crab recipes I discovered this simple and delicious one in Fortune Stanley's *English Country House Cooking*.

500 g	crabmeat	1 lb
3 tablespoons	butter	3 tablespoons
2 tablespoons	sherry	2 tablespoons
	salt, pepper	
1	small onion, chopped	1
6	mushrooms, sliced	6
3	red peppers, seeded and diced	3
3 tablespoons	tomato sauce or 1 tablespoon purée	3 tablespoons
1 tablespoon	single cream	1 tablespoon
2 tablespoons	browned breadcrumbs	2 tablespoons

Turn the crabmeat in half the hot butter over low heat, stir in the sherry and season.

Melt the remainder of the butter in a separate pan and cook the onion, mushrooms and red peppers. Stir in the crabmeat and tomato sauce mixed with the cream.

Turn into a hot serving dish and sprinkle with browned breadcrumbs. Serve very hot, with plain boiled rice or heart-shaped croûtons.

Smoked Whiting Florentine

Serves 4

Eggs, ham or, in this case, fish, served Florentine-style on a bed of nutmeg-flecked spinach and covered with a gentle béchamel sauce is a comforting and satisfying way of serving simple ingredients. Smoked whiting is cheaper than haddock and is, I think, more subtle.

4	smoked whiting fillets	4
¾ kg	fresh spinach	1½ lb
	or	
350 g	cooked or frozen spinach	12 oz
30 g	butter	1 oz
	grated nutmeg	

Béchamel sauce:

½ litre	milk	¾ pint
1	slice of onion	1
1	bay leaf	1
3	cloves	3
	salt, pepper	
45 g	butter	1½ oz
30 g	flour	1 oz
30 g	Parmesan cheese, finely grated	1 oz

Start the béchamel sauce first: heat the milk with the onion, bay leaf, cloves and a little salt and pepper and infuse over low heat for 15–30 minutes.

Meanwhile skin the fish with a sharp knife and arrange the fillets in a shallow dish or pan. Pour boiling water over them, cover and leave off the heat for 7 minutes.

Wash the fresh spinach and cook with a little salt in the water clinging to the leaves or prepare the frozen spinach as instructed on the packet. Strain and squeeze as free of water as possible. Reheat in a saucepan with the butter and freshly grated nutmeg to flavour. Keep hot.

Complete the sauce by melting the butter in a pan. Off-heat stir in the flour. Gradually whisk in the strained milk and cook, stirring, over moderate heat until thickened. (A béchamel sauce benefits from continuing to cook, over hot water, for up to 1 hour, if you are willing! It is often worth making a large quantity in this way for freezing.)

Now arrange the spinach in the base of one large or four individual oven dishes. Lift the fillets of fish from the hot water, drain thoroughly and place on top of the spinach. Pour the béchamel sauce over, scatter with Parmesan cheese and brown under a grill or in a hot oven.

Sometimes I add a little extra cheese to the sauce so that it becomes a Mornay sauce and heat as above.

Herrings à la Calaisienne
Serves 4

Cheap fresh herrings given an improving stuffing and cooked en papillote.

4	fresh herrings	4
	good knob of butter	
2 tablespoons	chopped parsley	2 tablespoons
60 g	chopped shallot	2 oz
60 g	mushrooms, finely chopped	2 oz
	squeeze of lemon juice	
	salt, pepper	
2	lemons, cut into wedges	2

Remove the heads and clean the fish. Split fully open and remove the roes. Place each fish skin side up on a board. Use the heel of your hand to push along the backbone from the tail to release the bones from the flesh. Turn over and pull off the backbone and any other bones.

Mash the roes in a bowl with the butter. Mix in the parsley, shallot, mushrooms and lemon juice with some salt and pepper.

Divide the stuffing between the fish and close the fish over it. Place the fish on a buttered sheet of foil, then fold over to make an envelope or wrap each fish separately.

Cook in a moderate oven, 180°C, 350°F, Gas Mark 4, for 15–20 minutes. Unwrap and serve with lemon quarters.

Russian Blini

Buckwheat has a flat, slightly bitter taste which combines admirably with soured cream, fish roe and lemon juice in this traditional Russian way. A good party food.

1 tablespoon	dried yeast	1 tablespoon
150 ml	warm water	¼ pint
150 ml	warm milk	¼ pint
180 g	buckwheat flour	6 oz
60 g	plain white flour	2 oz
½ teaspoon	salt	½ teaspoon
30 g	butter	1 oz
1 tablespoon	sugar	1 tablespoon
300 ml	warm milk	½ pint
2	eggs, separated	2
	clarified butter*	

For serving:

300 ml	soured cream	½ pint
1–2 pots	lump fish roe	1–2 pots
	or	
	caviare (if you've a Russian uncle)	
2	lemons, cut into wedges	2

In a large mixing bowl, sprinkle the yeast on to the warm water. Stir and leave in a warm place for 10 minutes to foam.

Use a balloon whisk to mix in the milk and three-quarters of both flours. Cover loosely with a plastic bag and set aside in a slightly warm place for 1–2 hours until double in bulk.

Add the salt, butter and sugar to the milk and stir until dissolved. Pour on to the egg yolks and mix into the yeast mixture with the rest of the flours.

Whisk the egg whites until stiff and fold into the mixture. Cover and leave in a warm place for half an hour, when the mixture will have risen again to regain its bulk.

Brush a small heavy-based frying pan or griddle with a little clarified butter and when really hot drop rounded tablespoons of the yeast mixture on to the pan. Start by taking the mixture from the side of the bowl only so that you leave the main surface of the yeast mixture undisturbed until you cook it.

Cook the blini, which should be about 8 cm (3 in) in diameter, on both sides until slightly golden (a blini is said to symbolise the sun and its return in the spring).

Serve the blini hot with soured cream, lumpfish roe or caviare and lemon wedges.

Blini freeze quite well but the real fun is in making them as you eat them. Any blini left over are nice eaten with jam or honey like English drop scones.

Clarified butter is pure fat, separated from the milk solids which turn butter rancid after too long exposure to air. Clarified butter has a higher burning point than other butter and is therefore excellent for frying and sautéing.

Heat unsalted butter over moderate heat until just melted. Skim off any froth from the surface and put aside. When the butter is clear, pour the yellow liquid into a bowl leaving the milky residue. The clarified butter will set hard and the milk solids left behind can be used in cakes and biscuits.

Soft Roes with Cider and Herbs *Serves 3–4*

Simplicity itself and so fine-flavoured: an excellent fish course or light meal.

500 g	soft herring roes	1 lb
30 g	seasoned flour	1 oz
45 g	butter	1½ oz
3–4 tablespoons	dry cider	3–4 tablespoons
1 tablespoon	chopped chives	1 tablespoon
1 tablespoon	chopped parsley	1 tablespoon
3–4 slices	hot toast	3–4 slices

Dip the soft roes in the seasoned flour in a plastic bag.

Melt the butter in a pan and gently fry the roes until lightly coloured. Remove the roes and keep hot.

Pour the cider into the pan and swill round to mix with the pan juices. Add the chives and parsley.

Divide the roes between the slices of toast and spoon over the sauce. Serve straight away.

Quenelles of Sea Bream
with Mushroom Sauce

Serves 4

Sea bream, also known as porgy, comes into season in early summer just as we are ready for lighter food. This kind of quenelle, as many restaurants have discovered, freezes well. So, if you like them, it is probably worth making a double quantity. Serve the freshly poached quenelles with mushroom sauce, Sauce Aurore or any other sauce suitable for fish.

250 g	sea bream, or whiting or monkfish fillets, skinned	8 oz
3 tablespoons	cold milk	3 tablespoons
120 g	white breadcrumbs	4 oz
60 g	unsalted butter	2 oz
1	egg	1
1	egg yolk	1
	salt, pepper	
2 teaspoons	finely chopped parsley or (optional) shrimps	2 teaspoons

Mushroom sauce:

45 g	butter	1½ oz
1	small onion, finely chopped	1
1	slim clove garlic, crushed	1
180 g	small mushrooms, quartered or sliced	6 oz
	salt, pepper	
20 g	flour	¾ oz
300 ml	creamy milk	½ pint
1–2 tablespoons	thick cream	1–2 tablespoons

Cut the fish into small pieces and check that every trace of bone has been removed. Purée the fish in a processor or mince it twice. Mix the milk with the breadcrumbs until it adheres and add to the processor with the butter, cut into pieces. Whizz to mix and then add the egg, egg yolk and some salt and pepper. I prefer to mix in a little finely chopped parsley or shrimps to relieve the creamy white look.

Spoon into a forcing bag fitted with a 1.5 cm (5/8 in) plain nozzle. Pipe the quenelles about 8 cm (3 in) long on to a sheet of greaseproof paper. If you prefer, simply shape the mixture into ovals with two dessertspoons. The quenelles can now be frozen; otherwise chill them until you are ready to cook.

Melt the butter in a pan and soften the onion and garlic. Add the mushrooms and cook together, stirring until they start to release their juices. Season with salt and pepper. Add the flour and stir for a minute or so. Pour in the milk gradually and cook, stirring, until thickened. Stir in the cream and keep the sauce hot until required.

Poach the quenelles in simmering salted water (or fish stock) for about 4 minutes or until cooked. Try one to test. Remove with a slotted spoon, drain on kitchen paper and transfer to a hot serving dish. Serve the quenelles with the sauce poured over them, accompanied by buttered rice.

Fishing Trip Matelote

Serves 6–8

An easy-going flexible recipe that comes into its own during the holidays—especially West Country ones where the fish, cider and cream are superb. Based on a Matelote Normande, I use whatever white fish bite at our lines or are good value at the fishmonger.

1 kg	assorted white fish—dabs, whiting, gurnard, sole, bream	2 lb
1	slice onion	1
1	bay leaf	1
	strip of lemon peel	
500 ml	water	¾ pint
30 g	butter	1 oz
2–3 tablespoons	Calvados or whisky (optional)	2–3 tablespoons
300 ml	dry cider	½ pint
	salt, pepper	
	bunch parsley stalks	
250 g	small mushrooms	8 oz
	knob of butter	
	squeeze of lemon juice	
1 tablespoon	each of butter and flour blended together to make beurre manié	1 tablespoon
120 g	clotted or double cream	4 oz
16	triangular croûtons toasted or fried	16
	few cooked prawns (optional)	
	chopped parsley	

Clean, fillet and skin the fish and cut the flesh into even sized pieces. Put all the bones and skin into a saucepan with the onion, bay leaf and lemon peel and water and simmer for 15 minutes to make a fish stock.

Melt the butter in a wide shallow pan and just stiffen the fish in it for 1–2 minutes. If including Calvados or whisky pour over and flame. Add the cider, strained fish stock, salt, pepper and the parsley stalks. Bring to the boil, then turn down the heat and cook gently until the fish is almost cooked. On no account overcook the fish.

Meanwhile cook the whole mushrooms in the knob of butter with the lemon juice and make the croûtons. If on holiday, get others to do this while you concentrate on the fish and its sauce.

Use a slotted spoon to lift the fish into a shallow serving dish and keep hot. Strain the liquor back into the pan and reduce a little over high heat. Thicken with the beurre manié, added in small pieces.

Finally stir in the cream, and pour the hot sauce (which should not be too thick) over the fish and arrange the mushrooms, croûtons and prawns around the fish. Dust with chopped parsley and serve straight away.

Russian Koulibiaka with Smoked Fish

Serves 4–8

Fillings for Koulibiaka can vary from fresh salmon to cabbage and hard-boiled egg. Here I opted for smoked fish and hard-boiled eggs with Jane Grigson's suggestion, from her *Fish Cookery*, of brown rice. I find the combination has a harmony which is pleasing. For Koulibiatski or small Koulibiaka cut the pastry into circles and gather the edges into the middle like a purse.

350 g	smoked haddock or whiting, boned	12 oz
60 g	butter	2 oz
3	spring onions, chopped	3
150 g	mushrooms, quartered	5 oz
	juice of ½ lemon	
	salt, pepper	
300 g	puff pastry, preferably home-made with butter	10 oz
120 g	brown rice, cooked	4 oz
2	hard-boiled eggs	2
1 teaspoon	fennel or dill seeds	1 teaspoon
2 tablespoons	chopped parsley	2 tablespoons
4 tablespoons	single cream	4 tablespoons
	egg yolk, to glaze	

Skin the fish and cut into ten or more neat pieces.

Melt the butter in a pan and gently cook the spring onions for a minute or so. Add the mushrooms and the lemon juice. When softened remove from the heat and season with salt and pepper.

Roll out the pastry and cut two rectangles about 30 × 18 cm (12×7 in). Place one piece on a baking sheet and spoon half the rice over it, leaving a good margin. Make a layer of mushrooms and cover with the fish and roughly chopped eggs. Sprinkle over the fennel or dill seeds and the parsley and the rest of the mushrooms. Finish with the rest of the rice and spoon over the cream.

Brush the margin of pastry with egg yolk and cover the filling with the other piece of pastry. Press the joins together well. Brush the top with egg yolk, make a steam vent and decorate with pieces of pastry from the trimmings.

Bake in the centre of a hot oven, 220°C, 425°F, Gas Mark 7, for about 30 minutes until golden and crisp. Slide the Koulibiaka on to a wooden board and serve as a first or main course.

To cook brown rice: have ready two cups of salted boiling water. Gradually add one cup of brown rice. Cover, lower the heat and cook for one hour.

Huss with Beurre Noir
and Three Vegetable Purées   *Serves 4*

Anyone over forty knows huss as rock salmon or eel, or as dog-fish in school laboratories. We dined on huss prepared this way in Carteret on the Cotentin peninsula. The purées complement the soft texture of the fish in an attractive fashion.

500 g	carrots, scraped and sliced	1 lb
500 g	celeriac or parsnip, peeled and sliced	1 lb
250 g	peas, fresh or frozen	8 oz
	salt, pepper	
¾ kg	huss, in four pieces	1½ lb
120 g	unsalted butter	4 oz
1 tablespoon	lemon juice or wine vinegar	1 tablespoon
1 tablespoon	chopped parsley	1 tablespoon

I prefer to use a steamer to cook this dish in two stages. Cook the carrots and celeriac, separated by a strip of foil, in the top half of a steamer until tender. Purée each vegetable separately and beat in a little of the butter and some salt and pepper. Cover the purées tightly and keep hot.

Now steam the fish, seasoned with salt and pepper, for 7–10 minutes or until cooked, and the peas, again separated by a wall of foil. (A friend tells me that with four Chinese steaming baskets all the cooking could be done at once, but I haven't yet tried it.) Remove the peas as soon as they are tender, purée as above and keep hot.

Melt the rest of the butter in a small pan and heat until the smell becomes nutty and the colour is golden brown. Carefully add the lemon juice or vinegar and pour the beurre noir over the fish arranged on hot plates. Sprinkle with parsley and place a spoonful of each purée neatly around the fish. Serve straight away.

EGGS
AND CHEESE

Eggs and cheese are the true convenience foods for budget gourmets. I find the so-called convenience foods—packet soups, packet pancake mix or desiccated curries—are only convenient for the manufacturer or shopkeeper. Cheap to produce, exceedingly light to transport and with a long shelf life, the cost per few grams or ounces is often higher than the same weight of salmon or caviare. Furthermore the poor taste and unwelcome additives consign this food to the junk class.

The taste of a lightly boiled fresh egg, served alone, with crusty bread and unsalted butter is a rare experience for many these days. And yet, this is simple food that should not be difficult to produce. But unless you have your own hens or can buy truly free-range eggs—note that the label 'farm eggs' does not mean the same thing—this is a cheap meal that is difficult to come by. When enough people really want good-tasting eggs they can be provided. It is cheering to hear that an egg farmer in the south-west is doing this. His free-range eggs are stamped with the date they are laid, not packed, an important difference. And they are selling well.

In total, however, national egg sales, compared with ten years ago, are down. Doubtless, this is in part due to the scare about the possibility that high-cholesterol containing foods could encourage heart disease.

Since we cannot yet be sure about this it seems sensible to urge, as in all things, moderation. In fact, eggs are a rich food and I find that one appears to limit one's consumption quite naturally. One can't also but wonder if the very cheapness of eggs has not cast a spell of economy over them which reduces their status and appeal.

Possibly one of the reasons that egg sales have fallen during the last few years is that we, sadly, have forgotten how to cook them imaginatively. There are hundreds of ways to cook eggs. Larousse gives over 300 and these don't include omelettes or soufflés. I hope that I have drawn attention to some ways that have been neglected or forgotten. Piperade, Pine Nut Omelette or Cocotte Eggs are all delicious, inexpensive and worth making frequently. Or make a sorrel purée to serve with a simply poached egg. Sorrel is no trouble to grow, even in a pot. Wash 120 g (4 oz) sorrel leaves and cook in the water clinging to them for 2–3 minutes until reduced and greeny-brown. Sieve into a bowl and beat in 75 g (2½ oz) unsalted butter cut in small pieces. Season and serve (it also freezes well).

Cheese is a highly underrated food. Like eggs, it has suffered from the bed-sit image. There are signs, however, that things are looking up. Not only are new cheeses being produced but the return to small scale cheese-making using cows', ewes' or goats' milk has focused attention on this splendid food.

Both Major Patrick Rance with his superb *The Great British Cheese Book* and Paxton and Whitfield's 'Cheese Club' (started two years ago and highly welcome to country dwellers) have played a part in re-establishing cheese as a respected food in this country. This influence is now affecting supermarkets and small High Street grocers so that genuine cheese rind is being seen again and the choice of uncut, unwrapped cheese is widening.

The French custom of serving cheese as part of the meal is excellent practice for budget gourmets. It allows the meat, fish or other protein course to be smaller and better, and, furthermore, enriches the taste experience of the whole meal. At times, cheese can stand on its own as the main course, in a Brioche de Gannat or in a superior rarebit, perhaps, while, at others, those happy companions, eggs and cheese together, can replace meat or fish.

Scrambled Eggs and Kidney   *Serves 2–4*

When I first knew my husband he lived in the top half of a
deadly sin, one of seven Edwardian houses overlooking the
Thames at Pangbourne and named so by the builder. He
cooked with the aid of *Venus in the Kitchen* (shouldn't we all)
by Pilaff Bey, the last book from Norman Douglas. This is one
of the simple yet delicious recipes.

4	lambs' kidneys	4
	knob of butter	
1 tablespoon	chopped parsley	1 tablespoon
3	tomatoes, peeled and chopped	3
	salt, pepper	
3–4	eggs, beaten	3–4

Skin the kidneys, remove the core and cut into thin slices.

Melt the butter in a pan and cook the kidneys gently with
the parsley. After 1–2 minutes, add the tomatoes and some
salt and pepper.

Cook everything for 4–5 minutes. Then pour in the beaten
eggs and scramble them, stirring now and again, until cooked.

Brioche de Gannat filled with Melon and Tomato Salad   *Serves 8*

This cheese brioche from the Auvergne is properly made with Cantal cheese but Gruyère or Cheddar work well. In winter try making the brioche with Stilton and serve it hot with soups.

250 g	plain flour	8 oz
60 ml	warm water	2 fl oz
15 g	fresh yeast	½ oz
	or	
1 teaspoon	dried yeast	1 teaspoon
60 ml	milk	2 fl oz
60 g	butter	2 oz
2	eggs, beaten	2
120 g	grated cheese (see above)	4 oz
Salad:		
350 g	ripe fleshy tomatoes	12 oz
1	small ripe melon	1
	chopped chives	
150 ml	Sauce Vinaigrette	¼ pint
1	bunch watercress	1

Sieve the flour into a bowl and set aside in a warm place. Measure the water into a cup and add the yeast, crumbling or sprinkling it into the water. Stir and leave to foam for 10 minutes.

Meanwhile warm the milk with the butter until just melted. Make a well in the middle of the flour. Add the foamed yeast, buttery milk and eggs and mix all together well until it forms a soft dough. Knead on a floured surface for 5 minutes until elastic.

Return the dough to the bowl and cover with a loose plastic bag. Set in a warm place until double in bulk.

Turn the dough on to a floured board and knead in the cheese. Roll into a sausage shape to fit a well-buttered 20 cm (8 in) ring cake tin. Allow to prove for 10–15 minutes or until the dough is level with the rim of the tin.

Bake in the centre of a hot oven, 200°C, 400°F, Gas Mark 6, for 30–35 minutes or until the brioche is just shrinking from the tin. Leave in the tin for 5 minutes, then turn out on to a wire rack.

Peel the tomatoes and quarter. Deseed the melon and scoop out the flesh with a melon baller. Layer the tomatoes and melon in a bowl with the chopped chives, pour over the Sauce Vinaigrette and leave for 30 minutes.

Place the brioche on a flat dish. Arrange crisp watercress around the outside and fill the centre with the salad. Serve the salad together with a wedge of brioche.

Cocotte Eggs with Smoked Cod's Roe

Serves 4

A particularly happy combination, I find. This is one of my favourite light dishes for eating while breadmaking. Easily cooked on the floor of the oven, serve one egg each as a first course or double up for a light meal.

30 g	unsalted butter	1 oz
4 tablespoons	smoked cod's roe	4 tablespoons
4	large new-laid eggs	4
	salt, pepper	
4 tablespoons	single cream or top of milk	4 tablespoons
	sprigs of parsley	

Heat 4 cocotte dishes and add a little butter to each. As the butter melts, run it across the base.

Place 1 tablespoon of smoked cod's roe in each cocotte dish and break an egg on top. Season with salt and freshly milled pepper. Add 1 tablespoon of cream to each dish and divide the rest of the butter between them.

Place the dishes in a bain-marie and cook on the base of a hot oven, 200°C, 400°F, Gas Mark 6, until the white of egg is set but the yolk is still soft, about 5–8 minutes.

Alternatively, cook in a covered pan of hot water to come half-way up the dishes, again for about 5–8 minutes. Arrange a sprig of parsley on each—the flat parsley tastes and looks best. Serve with crusty French bread.

Oeufs au Printemps

Serves 6

A pretty first course for an Easter meal.

6	hard-boiled eggs	6
90 g	cream cheese	3 oz
	a little top of milk	
1 tablespoon	finely chopped chives	1 tablespoon
	salt, pepper	
1	bunch of watercress	1
	few leaves of young spinach	
2–3 tablespoons	finely chopped parsley	2–3 tablespoons
150 ml	mild mayonnaise, home-made or Sainsbury's French	¼ pint
	a squeeze of lemon	
	few leaves for garnish, lettuce or watercress	

Halve the eggs lengthways and remove the yolks. Set one yolk aside, covered, for the garnish.

Work the yolks and the cream cheese together in a bowl with a little top of milk. When smooth, mix in the chives and season with salt and pepper.

Spoon the mixture back into the whites of egg and sandwich the halves together to re-form.

Blanch the watercress and spinach in boiling water for 1 minute. Drain and refresh under cold water. Squeeze free of water and pat dry on a cloth. Chop finely or process.

Mix the watercress and spinach with the chopped parsley into the mayonnaise. Sharpen to taste with lemon juice.

Spoon the green mayonnaise over the stuffed eggs. Garnish with small leaves of lettuce or watercress and rub the reserved egg yolk through a nylon sieve over the eggs to resemble mimosa.

Home-made Egg Pasta

Serves 3–4

One of the most satisfying dishes to make at home. Pasta dough is beautiful to handle and is endlessly versatile—cut to shape, tucked or rolled, pinched or pushed around so many fillings that the challenge to continue devising dishes always remains.

On the advice of the Camisa family of Fratelli Camisa in Berwick Street, Soho, whose own fresh pasta is always tempting, I use one-third fine semolina and two-thirds durum flour as in the recipe below. If these are difficult to obtain, use strong white bread flour instead.

Basic recipe for pasta gialla:

75 g	fine semolina	2½ oz
150 g	durum flour	5 oz
	or	
215 g	white bread flour	7½ oz
2	large eggs	2

Work on a wooden or plastic surface or in a wide shallow bowl. Make a well in the centre of the dry ingredients and add the slightly beaten eggs. With your hand or a wooden spoon gradually draw the flour into the centre and mix with the eggs until the dough forms a ball.

Alternatively break the eggs into a processor or mixer bowl and gradually add the dry ingredients until the dough forms a ball. I find, however, that making pasta by hand gives a better result.

On a floured surface knead the dough, as for bread, for 5–10 minutes, depending upon the heat of your kitchen and your energy. The dough should now be smooth and elastic.

Use a long straight rolling pin to roll the dough, stretching it away from you as you work. After each roll turn the dough through 90°, and roll out the dough until 3 mm (⅛ in) thick.

Finally roll the dough until it is thin enough to see through. The best technique here is to work on the further half of the dough each time. Roll a quarter of the dough furthest from you around the rolling pin. Now roll out the dough, moving the pin towards and away from you in quick movements, smoothing your hands, with fingers splayed, along the rolling pin and back to the centre all the time to distribute the pressure evenly while stretching the dough.

Unroll, turn the dough by a quarter and repeat. You will find that the dough is very strong and supple and there is no likelihood of tearing. When the whole sheet has been thinned, drape the dough on a cloth over a table, allowing one third to hang down. After 10 minutes rotate one third, repeat after 10 minutes. The dough should then be dry enough to cut.

Fold up into a flat roll and cut to whichever width you prefer. For *tagliatelle* cut the pasta 6 mm (¼ in) wide, for *fettucine* cut the pasta 3 mm (⅛ in) wide. Separate the strips, dry for about 5 minutes and then cook in boiling salted water until *al dente*, i.e. with just a hint of bite. Serve with unsalted butter, sea salt, milled black pepper and freshly grated Parmesan cheese or any suitable sauce.

If you don't wish to cook all the pasta at this stage, let it dry thoroughly, then store in a cool, dry cupboard for up to one month. The drier it becomes the longer it will take to cook.

To make pasta rosa:
Add 2 teaspoons tomato paste to the basic recipe with the eggs.
To make pasta verde:
Replace 1 egg white in the basic recipe with about 2 table-spoons sieved cooked spinach.

If you have access to fresh basil by growing your own or have a good market near, you won't want to waste the opportunity to make Pesto, the Genoese basil sauce for pasta and soup.

Here is Marcella Hazan's recipe for making Pesto in a blender or processor.

Pesto

100 g	fresh basil leaves	3½ oz
8 tablespoons	olive oil	8 tablespoons
30 g	pine nuts	1 oz
2	cloves of garlic, lightly crushed	2
	salt	
50 g	Parmesan cheese, freshly grated	1¾ oz
2 tablespoons	Romano *pecorino* cheese, freshly grated	2 tablespoons
40 g	butter, softened	1½ oz

Put the basil (take care not to crush it while handling), olive oil, pine nuts, garlic and salt in the blender and mix at high speed. Check from time to time that all the mixture is being blended.

Add the cheeses by hand and then beat in the butter.

When ready to serve add a tablespoon or so of the hot water in which the pasta has boiled.

I find it is not always easy to track down the Romano cheese out of London, in which case add just a little more Parmesan instead. If you wish to freeze this sauce, omit the cheeses and butter and add them when the sauce has thawed.

Spinach Roulade with Rosy Cockles

Serves 4–6

A spinach soufflé cooked flat and then rolled up like a swiss roll, round a sauce of cockles with paprika. If you've had little success with soufflés, try this rather easier style.

2 tablespoons	Parmesan cheese, finely grated	2 tablespoons
500 g	fresh spinach	1 lb
	or	
200 g	frozen spinach	7 oz
	salt, pepper	
	grated nutmeg	
15 g	butter	½ oz
4	eggs, separated	4

Sauce:

20 g	butter	¾ oz
1 teaspoon	sweet paprika	1 teaspoon
15 g	flour	½ oz
150 ml	creamy milk	¼ pint
1	spring onion, finely chopped	1
1 tablespoon	chopped parsley	1
120 g	cockles, well washed	4 oz
2–3	small pickled gherkins	2–3
	salt, pepper	
2–3 tablespoons	thick cream	2–3 tablespoons

Butter a 33×23 cm (13×9 in) swiss roll tin and line with non-stick silicone paper. Lift the paper, turn over and smooth into the tin again. Scatter half the Parmesan cheese over the paper.

Strip the stems from the spinach and wash the leaves. Cook in the water clinging to the leaves with a little salt until tender. Drain well and chop finely by hand or in a processor.

If using frozen spinach, cook (still frozen) with no extra water over moderate heat until thawed. Chop the spinach and return to the heat, stirring all the time, until all the surplus moisture has been evaporated.

Season the spinach with plenty of grated nutmeg and stir in the butter and egg yolks while the spinach is still warm. Fold in the stiffly whisked egg whites.

Turn the mixture into the prepared tin and spread level. Sprinkle with the remaining cheese.

Cook in the centre of a moderate oven, 190°C, 375°F, Gas Mark 5, for 10–15 minutes until firm but springy, and the cheese is just changing colour.

Meanwhile make the sauce. Melt the butter and stir in the paprika for ½ minute and then the flour. Gradually whisk in the milk and cook, stirring, until thickened.

Add the onion, parsley, cockles and gherkins. Season to taste. Leave over low heat to cook slowly. Just before serving stir in the cream.

Turn the roulade out on to a sheet of paper and peel off the silicone paper. Pour the sauce over the roulade and use the paper to roll up from the narrow end.

Turn on to a hot serving dish with the join at the base. Serve straight away, cut into thick slices.

Poached Eggs in Wine Sauce   *Serves 3–6*

An Italian version, using white wine, of the Burgundian red wine dish Oeufs en Meurette. I reckon that the cheapness of the eggs offsets the cost of the wine. The recipe, slightly adapted, is from Wilma Pezzini's *Tuscan Cookbook*.

300 ml	dry white wine, preferably Italian or ½ wine/½ water	½ pint
2	medium onions, quartered	2
2	cloves garlic, crushed	2
1	bay leaf	1
	salt, pepper	
6	eggs	6
6	slices white bread	6
2 tablespoons	butter	2 tablespoons
1–2 tablespoons	flour	1–2 tablespoons

Measure the wine into a wide saucepan with the onions, garlic, bay leaf and a little salt and pepper. Bring to the boil and simmer very gently for about 10 minutes.

Poach the eggs one or two at a time in the wine. Alternatively, poach the eggs in acidulated water while the wine reduces.

Remove the crusts from the bread and either fry in extra butter or, as I prefer, toast lightly. Blend the butter with the flour and add to the wine in small pieces. Cook, stirring, until thickened.

Place an egg on each slice of toast and strain the wine sauce over.

Lymeswold Soufflé

Serves 3–4

In the battery of criticism of Lymeswold cheese most people have overlooked the point that it has happened at all. A small cheer for Dairy Crest who reckon we need to boost our cheese industry. Other blue cheeses, such as Stilton, Dolcelatte or Cambazola (an influence on Lymeswold, I gather) also make a very good soufflé.

1½ tablespoons	white breadcrumbs, baked until golden	1½ tablespoons
30 g	butter	1 oz
15 g	flour	½ oz
150 ml	milk	¼ pint
90 g	Lymeswold cheese, diced	3 oz
¼ teaspoon	dry mustard	¼ teaspoon
	grated nutmeg	
	salt, pepper	
3	egg yolks	3
4	egg whites	4

Butter a 1.25 litre (2 pint) soufflé dish and dust with the browned breadcrumbs.

Melt the butter in a heavy based pan and add the flour, stirring for 1 minute. Gradually whisk in the milk and cook, stirring, until thickened.

Add the cheese, mustard, nutmeg, a little salt and some pepper. Cook for 2 minutes, stirring until the cheese has melted.

Beat in the egg yolks and cook, gently, for 1–2 minutes until slightly thickened. Remove from heat.

Whisk the egg whites until stiff. Fold some into the cheese sauce. Then pour the sauce into the egg whites, folding as you do so.

Turn into the prepared dish and bake in a hot oven, 220°C, 425°F, Gas Mark 7, for 12–15 minutes until well risen and golden brown. A glass oven door is a tremendous asset here.

Carry the soufflé carefully to the table and serve straight away on to hot plates.

Cheese and Caraway Triangles

Makes about 18 biscuits

Potato pastry makes good biscuits for serving with soup or a salad. The pastry recipe comes from *The Home Book of Viennese Cookery* by Trude Johnston.

180 g	cooked potato, sieved and cooled	6 oz
120 g	plain flour	4 oz
120 g	margarine or butter	4 oz
1	egg yolk	1
¼ teaspoon	salt	¼ teaspoon
1–2 tablespoons	grated Cheddar cheese	1–2 tablespoons
1 teaspoon	caraway seeds	1 teaspoon

In a bowl work the potato, flour and margarine or butter into a dough with almost all the egg yolk mixed with the salt.

On a floured board roll out the pastry to ½ cm (¼ in) thickness. Brush with the rest of the egg yolk and sprinkle with the cheese and the caraway seeds. Cut into triangles and bake on a greased baking sheet in a moderate oven, 190°C, 375°F, Gas Mark 5, for about 15 minutes until puffed up and golden. Serve hot or cold.

Piperade

Twenty-five years ago this was the first dish from Elizabeth David that I cooked, and it is still a great favourite. Now that so many of our green peppers are home-grown they are much cheaper. As a compromise and because it looks lovely, I use some green peppers and some red.

1–2 tablespoons	pork or bacon fat	1–2 tablespoons
500 g	onions, sliced	1 lb
3	large sweet red peppers	3
	or	
6	smaller green peppers	6
500 g	large ripe tomatoes, sliced	1lb
	salt, pepper	
	a little marjoram, chopped	
6	eggs, beaten	6

Melt the fat in a wide, heavy based pan. Cook the onions slowly until golden but not brown.

Remove the seeds from the peppers and slice. Add to the pan and cook until soft.

Cover with the sliced tomatoes and season with salt, pepper and the marjoram.

Cook, covered, until as soft as a purée; if the tomatoes are watery you may have to remove the lid during the cooking to evaporate some of the moisture.

When the mixture is soft all through, pour in the eggs and stir gently as for scrambled eggs.

Serve as soon as the egg has set. An excellent accompaniment to Brochette of Calves' Liver. (See p. 173).

Melting Camembert
with Crab Apple Jelly

Serves 4

The cheese can be prepared ahead, and even frozen if preferred, to be cooked just before serving.

1	Camembert cheese, whole or in portions	1
1	egg, beaten	1
	fine white breadcrumbs	
	clarified butter (see p. 64)	
	crab apple or grape jelly	

Cut the cheese into quarters. Brush each piece with beaten egg and roll in breadcrumbs. Chill or freeze the cheese until needed.

Melt some clarified butter in a pan and shallow fry the cheese until golden on all sides.

Serve with a little crab apple or other slightly sharp homemade jelly. The cheese should have a crisp crust and be soft and melting inside.

Scotch Woodcock with Poached Eggs

Serves 4

A traditional savoury course that is rarely seen in domestic cookery these days, but well worth reviving as a light meal.

120 g	unsalted butter	4 oz
30 g	flour	1 oz
300 ml	boiling water	½ pint
	salt, pepper	
	juice of ½ lemon	
2 tablespoons	capers	2 tablespoons
50 g	tin anchovy fillets	1¾ oz
4	slices fresh bread	4
4	freshly poached eggs	4

Make the butter sauce first. Melt 30 g (1oz) of the butter in a small heavy based pan and stir in the flour to make a roux. Gradually whisk in the water and cook for 4–5 minutes until the sauce has thickened and is smooth.

Remove from the heat and season with salt and pepper. Cool the pan a little and then beat in the rest of the butter, cut into small pieces, added gradually with drops of lemon juice. The sauce will thicken and turn opaque. Keep the sauce warm over hot, though not boiling, water.

Rinse the capers under cold water to rid them of vinegar, then drain and dry on a cloth. Add them to the sauce. Separate the anchovy fillets and quickly rinse in cold water.

Lightly toast the bread and remove the crusts. Place each slice on a hot plate. Pour butter sauce over each slice of toast, place an egg on each and arrange the anchovy fillets, criss-cross on top.

Pop under a very hot grill for one minute, then serve straight away.

Croque Monsieur

A Gallic version of a toasted cheese sandwich bathed in a cheese sauce. The better the ham the more delicious the dish.

8	slices white bread	8
4	slices ham	4
	a little Dijon mustard	
250 g	Gruyère cheese	8 oz
60 g	butter	2 oz
30 g	flour	1 oz
300 ml	warm milk	½ pint
½ teaspoon	dried herbs or grated onion	½ teaspoon
2	eggs	2
	cayenne pepper or chopped parsley	

Cut the crusts from the bread and cover four slices with ham spread with a little mustard. Slice or grate half the cheese over the ham.

Press the rest of the bread on top to make four sandwiches. Leave whole or cut across into triangles.

Melt 45 g (1½ oz) of the butter in a pan and stir in the flour. Gradually whisk in the milk and cook, stirring, until thickened. Add the rest of the cheese, grated, and the herbs or onion to the sauce and keep hot.

Beat the eggs and pour into a shallow dish. Dip both sides of each sandwich in the egg and fry in the rest of the butter until crisp and golden.

Serve the Croque Messieurs on very hot plates with the sauce poured across them and sprinkle with cayenne pepper or chopped parsley.

Variation: Croque Madame is made with chicken instead of ham.

Potted Stilton

Perhaps the best refuge for the last vestige of a Stilton cheese; a good January standby. Serve as a cheese course or in sauces.

500 g	mature Stilton cheese	1 lb
200 g	unsalted butter	7 oz
	a small glass of port	

Shave away the rind from the cheese and grate or finely chop the cheese itself.

Soften the butter in a bowl and gradually work in the cheese. Beat in the port until you are satisfied with the flavour. Spoon into small pots and cover.

The potted cheese will keep up to a month in a refrigerator and up to 4 months in the freezer.

Toasted Goat Cheese and Chicory *Serves 4*

We were in London the day my husband celebrated his half century so I took him to dinner at the Dorchester to sample Anton Mosimann's delectable cuisine. This was the cheese course, served with walnut bread.

100 g	goat cheese	3½ oz
1 head	Belgian chicory	1 head
	few leaves radicchio	
	walnut oil	

Divide the goat cheese between four plates, giving each person two slices. Toast under a hot grill until the surface is just starting to colour.

Arrange 2 or 3 leaves of chicory beside the cheese and a leaf or so of radicchio. Dribble a little walnut oil over the leaves. Serve at once.

Pine Nut Omelette

Pine nuts, best bought in wholefood shops and kept in the fridge or freezer, really can give zest to your cooking. Here they add an exciting taste and texture. This is a perfect example of how good cooking is always more than the sum of its parts.

> 1 teaspoon olive oil
> 1 tablespoon pine nuts
> 2 or 3 eggs
> salt, pepper
> ½ clove garlic
> small knob of butter
> 1 tablespoon chopped parsley
> good squeeze of lemon juice

Heat the oil in a small omelette pan and sauté the pine nuts until golden brown and the flavour is released. Scoop the nuts on to a hot serving dish and keep hot.

Break the eggs into a bowl. Season with salt and pepper and lightly beat with a fork spiked with the garlic.

Add the butter to the pan and heat until bubbling. Pour in the eggs and use the blade of a knife to gently lift the edges of the omelette to let surplus liquid egg run underneath.

As soon as some of the egg has set but is still liquid on top, sprinkle with chopped parsley. Arrange the pine nuts along the central third of the omelette and squeeze lemon juice over them.

Flip first one and then the other side of the omelette over the nuts. Quickly turn the omelette on to the hot serving plate and eat straight away.

John Arlott's Lancashire Rarebit

Serves 2–4

I had already typed out for this chapter my Devonshire version of Welsh Rarebit which includes local cider when John Arlott's recipe arrived with cheese notes from Paxton and Whitfield. We tried it and in the rarebit (from 'rearbit' or food taken at the end of the meal) contest it was pronounced a winner.

4	slices thin, buttered, trimmed toast	4
60 g	butter	2 oz
250 g	Lancashire cheese	8 oz
300 ml	beer	½ pint
2	egg yolks	2
2 tablespoons	made mustard	2 tablespoons
	2 dashes Worcester sauce	
	shake paprika and cayenne pepper	

Keep the toast warm while you make the sauce.

Melt the butter in a pan and crumble the cheese into it. Slowly stir in the beer and the egg yolks mixed with the mustard, Worcester sauce, paprika and cayenne pepper.

Cook together for a minute then pour over each slice of toast and place under a hot grill until gently browned.

Summer Herb Tart

Serves 6

Beg, barter or borrow fresh herbs for this beautiful green tart. Buying fresh herbs is not always easy. Local markets and WI stalls are usually the best bet, but Waitrose sell trays of mixed herbs—let's hope other shops follow. Often children, or weekend guests who like to use the kitchen as a confessional, are willing to de-stalk and chop the herbs.

150 g	plain flour	5 oz
	pinch of salt	
90 g	unsalted butter	3 oz
1	egg yolk mixed with	1
1 tablespoon	milk	1 tablespoon
2	eggs	2
2	egg yolks	2
generous 150 ml	single cream	generous ¼ pint
60 g	mixed fresh herbs—parsley, chives, chervil, tarragon— finely chopped	2 oz
	salt, pepper	

Sieve the flour and salt into a bowl and rub in the butter. Mix to a dough with the egg yolk and milk. Chill the dough, wrapped, for half an hour.

Roll out to fit a buttered 23 cm (9 in) flan tin. Prick the base and bake in a moderately hot oven, 200°C, 400°F, Gas Mark 6, for 10–15 minutes until the pastry is set but not coloured. Remove the case and lower the oven to 190°C, 375°F, Gas Mark 5.

Beat the eggs and egg yolks with the cream. Stir in the herbs and some salt and pepper. Pour into the slightly cooled pastry case and bake on a baking sheet for a further 20–25 minutes, until the filling is set. Serve hot, warm or cold.

VEGETABLES

I derive immense satisfaction, a positive thrill, from growing, selecting and cooking vegetables—probably because I enjoy eating them so much. For me, a beautifully cooked and presented vegetable is a matter of pride, and is a dish worthy of its own place on the menu. I much favour serving a vegetable as a separate course, thereby according it some status on the menu, instead of treating it as always the brides-maid to the main course in a meal. Generally, only asparagus is treated this way and, one suspects, that has as much to do with its price as its taste. If asparagus were as cheap as runner beans it would most likely be chopped up and served, over-cooked, like any other vegetable, in a sad heap beside the meat.

I suggest that we don't let the rules of the marketplace blind us to the true taste of vegetables. When picked very young—no longer than your fingers, even runner beans, cooked gently and served whole with maître d'hotel butter, are almost as delicious as asparagus, at a quarter of the price.

But still, the spectre of the show-bench stalks the kitchen garden and allotment. Recently, when I complimented a (bon vivant) friend on a bowl of tiny home-grown brussels sprouts and finger-width leeks, he blamed the weather for his poor results. But they taste much better this size, I protested. He seemed unconvinced. Small is not yet thought beautiful in the vegetable kingdom.

It makes sense financially and gastronomically to eat vege-tables with the seasons. Of course, if you grow or have access to cheap supplies of fine vegetables it is probably worth freezing some. But only freeze the most tender and succulent: broad beans, mangetout and French beans survive well, I find. Overdependence on frozen vegetables, however, deprives one of the excitement of enjoying the first baby carrots or the earliest sugar-sweet peas. These first fruits of the season are best served simply, with just a knob of butter and a sprinkling of sea salt.

Later on, when vegetables become more plentiful and cheaper, it is rewarding to be more adventurous. I like to serve vegetables in combination: perhaps some chopped spinach bathed in a mushroom and coriander sauce, or narrow boats of courgettes filled with a purée of broad beans. Try preparing a selection of vegetables ratatouille-style, cooked gently between layers of sliced tomatoes.

All vegetables are easily ruined by thoughtless cooking. Steaming is frequently preferable to boiling. Not only are the texture and flavour superior but fewer vitamins are thrown away in the cooking water. I use a metal collapsible basket or a bamboo steaming basket. Even a colander or a metal sieve will work if you place a plate at the bottom. A few years ago I bought a cheap cous-cousière in a French hypermarket and this is invaluable for steaming larger quantities.

Some vegetables, such as turnip, swede or salsify, benefit from braising in liquids other than water—stock, yoghurt, milk or in a sauce or even gravy, perhaps. 'Gravy and potatoes in a good brown pot, Put them in the oven and serve them very hot!'

Grilled or barbecued vegetables are a great treat, brushed with oil or butter to keep them moist; try green and red peppers, courgettes, broccoli and baby carrots this way. Anton Mosimann suggests marinàding them in oil for 30 minutes first.

Crisp roast potatoes and parsnips cooked around a joint of meat are a delight in winter, for me, only just surpassed by jacket potatoes, halved and running with butter and black pepper. On the whole the humble spud does not receive quite the imaginative treatment meted out to other vegetables, so I have included several ways of cooking it.

Let us not forget that many vegetables are splendid for stuffing with savoury mixtures of meat, fish or rice. Or indeed, themselves. I once stuffed a large green pepper with a slightly smaller red pepper and in turn with a yellow pepper and at last a green chilli pepper, all of them separated by a thin sheet of cheese and cooked en papillote. It tasted very good indeed and looked fun when cut in half lengthways. Such dishes are excellent hot or cold. Once you start looking afresh at vegetables the possibilities are endless.

Stuffed Mushrooms

Serves 4

With luck, in mushroom country, September's heavy dews encourage the still warm earth to produce *Agaricus campestris*, the large flat field mushroom. Due to their perishable nature field mushrooms are usually very cheap and, of course, even more so if you pick your own. Some shops are now selling large flat cultivated mushrooms all year round, but, so far at any rate, they are quite dear.

8	large flat mushrooms	8
	knob of butter	
1	clove garlic or small onion	1
350 g	best sausage meat	12 oz
1 teaspoon	chopped fresh thyme	1 teaspoon
	salt, pepper	
8	walnut halves (optional) or black olives	8
2–3 tablespoons	white wine or stock	2–3 tablespoons

Use a damp cloth to wipe the mushrooms (only peel if really necessary) and remove the stalks.

Arrange the tops, gill side up, in a single layer in a buttered oven dish.

Chop the mushroom stalks and mix with the finely chopped garlic or onion and the sausage meat. Season with salt and pepper.

Spoon the stuffing on to each mushroom and shape into a mound with the prongs of a fork. Press a half walnut or olive on top of each mushroom. Pour wine or stock into the dish and bake in a moderately hot oven, 200°C, 400°F, Gas Mark 6, for 20–30 minutes or until cooked.

Cauliflower with Whiskied Carrots

Serves 4

Perhaps an unusual combination of vegetables, but they harmonise well this way.

1	medium cauliflower	1
350 g	carrots	12 oz
	salt, pepper	
30 g	unsalted butter	1 oz
4 tablespoons	single cream	4 tablespoons
2 tablespoons	whisky	2 tablespoons
	finely chopped chives or parsley	

Trim the stalk and leaves of the cauliflower and divide into 4, through the stem, for cooking. Soak in cold salted water.

Peel and slice the carrots.

Steam the cauliflower until just cooked and cook the carrots in salted water until tender. Strain the carrots, turn into a processor or blender with the butter and whizz to a purée. Alternatively (and better) sieve or mash the carrots and return to the pan.

Season with pepper and beat in the cream and whisky over low heat.

Arrange the cooked cauliflower on a hot serving dish and spoon the whiskied carrots over the stem ends. Sprinkle the cauliflower with finely chopped chives or parsley and serve.

Okra with Tomatoes

Serves 4–6

Tomatoes provide a splendid medium in which to cook other vegetables. Cooked in Greek style with okra, or Ladies' Fingers, the resulting sauce is thick and fruity due to the juice from the okra. It can also be served as a first course.

500 g	ripe tomatoes	1 lb
500 g	fresh okra	1 lb
3 tablespoons	olive oil	3 tablespoons
1	bunch spring onions, chopped	1
1	clove garlic, crushed	1
	juice of 1 lemon	
½ teaspoon	sugar	½ teaspoon
	salt, pepper	
	chopped fresh parsley or chervil	

Skin the tomatoes by immersing in boiling water for 10 seconds and then in cold water. Nick the skins with a sharp knife and they will slide off easily. Chop roughly and set aside.

Wash and dry the okra and cut away the stalk on each one as close to the pod as you can without exposing the seeds.

Heat the oil in a wide shallow pan and cook the onions and garlic gently for 2–3 minutes. Draw the onions to one side of the pan and gently sauté the okra for about 5 minutes, turning them now and again. Stir the onions and garlic into the okra and add the tomatoes, lemon juice, sugar and some salt and pepper.

Bring to the boil, turn down the heat and simmer gently for 20–25 minutes so that the okra remain whole and the tomatoes reduce to a thick sauce.

Turn into a white shallow dish for maximum impact and sprinkle with chopped parsley.

Parsnips au Gratin

Serves 4

One of the simplest of parsnip dishes but one of the best. As a child during post-war austerity Britain, this was one of my favourite dishes.

¾ kg	sound, firm parsnips	1½ lb
	a splash of milk	
	salt	
45 g	butter	1½ oz
	grated nutmeg	
120–180 g	sliced Cheddar or Gruyère cheese	4–6 oz

Scrape or peel the parsnips thinly and cut into ½ cm (¼ in) rounds. Barely cover with cold water, the milk and some salt and bring to the boil. Cook until just tender.

Drain and arrange in a buttered gratin dish. Dot with butter and grate some nutmeg over the top. Cover with thinly sliced cheese.

Bake in a hot oven or place under the grill until the cheese melts and the top is golden brown.

A variation is *parsnip galette*. Cook about 1 kg (2 lb) parsnips as above. Arrange the sliced, cooked parsnips in an 18 cm (7 in) buttered cake tin, layer with the cheese and some chopped spring onions and bake in a moderate oven, 180°C, 350°F, Gas Mark 4, for 30–40 minutes until welded together. Turn out on to a hot plate and cut into wedges.

Potato Daube

With a wry smile of recognition I recently discovered this dish that I had devised (I thought) and have been cooking for years, in Richard Olney's *Simple French Food*. Perhaps cooks have a collective subconscious. This is a cheap, wholesome and delicious way of cooking potatoes.

4	cloves of garlic, peeled	4
300 ml	water	½ pint
	salt, pepper	
¾ kg	waxy potatoes like Desirée	1½ lb
2–3 tablespoons	olive oil	2–3 tablespoons
3	bay leaves, halved, fresh if possible	3

Slice the cloves of garlic into a pan and simmer, covered, in the water with some salt for about 10 minutes.

Meanwhile peel the potatoes and slice thinly. Brush a casserole with olive oil and place half a bay leaf on the base. Arrange the potatoes and the rest of the bay leaves in layers with a little more salt and some pepper. Strain the garlic water through a sieve (push through the garlic too, if you wish) on to the potatoes. Spoon over the rest of the olive oil and cover tightly.

Cook in a moderate oven, 190°C, 375°F, Gas Mark 5, for 45 minutes. The potatoes absorb the water and you end up with potatoes in a thin garlic sauce.

Walnut and Carrot Tart

Serves 6–8

A robust vegetarian lunch or supper dish, also ideal for packed lunches.

Walnut oat pastry:

90 g	broken walnuts	3 oz
60 g	medium oatmeal	2 oz
90 g	plain flour, white or wholemeal	3 oz
½ teaspoon	ground cinnamon	½ teaspoon
½ teaspoon	salt	½ teaspoon
45 g	butter or margarine	1½ oz
2–3 tablespoons	hot water	2–3 tablespoons

Filling:

250 g	carrots	8 oz
1	clove garlic, crushed	1
1	stick celery, finely chopped	1
2	eggs	2
4 tablespoons	top of milk	4 tablespoons
	salt, pepper	
2–3 tablespoons	apple, quince or redcurrant jelly	2–3 tablespoons

Chop the walnuts, not too finely, in a processor or blender. Tip into a bowl and stir in the oatmeal, flour, cinnamon and salt. Melt the butter in the hot water and pour on to the dry ingredients. Mix to a soft dough.

Roll out on a floured surface to fit a greased 20–23 cm (8–9 in) flat tin.

Grate the carrots finely and mix with the garlic, celery, eggs and milk. Season with salt and pepper. Turn the filling into the pastry case and bake on a metal sheet in a moderately hot oven, 190°C, 375°F, Gas Mark 5, for about 30 minutes until the pastry is crisp and the filling is set.

Remove from the oven and brush the jelly over the filling. Cut into wedges and serve hot or cold with a salad.

Potato Croquettes

Serves 4

Much more appetising than chips in my view. I like to double or treble the quantities because they freeze so well and can be cooked from frozen.

¾ kg	potatoes, peeled	1½ lb
30 g	butter	1 oz
2	egg yolks	2
2–3 tablespoons	milk	2–3 tablespoons
2 tablespoons	finely chopped chives or parsley	2 tablespoons
	salt, pepper	
	a little flour	
1	egg, beaten	1
½ teacup	dry white breadcrumbs	½ teacup
	deep fat for frying	

Boil the potatoes in salted water until cooked. Drain well and replace the pan over the heat to dry them thoroughly.

Using a sieve or mouli-légumes, finely sieve the potatoes into a warm bowl. Mix in the butter, egg yolks, milk and chopped chives. Season to taste with salt and pepper.

Turn the mixture on to a floured board and, when cool, divide into about 16 pieces. Roll each piece into a sausage. Roll in flour, dip in beaten egg and then roll in breadcrumbs. Open freeze at this stage, if desired.

Deep fry the potato croquettes, thawed or frozen, in hot fat until golden brown. Drain on kitchen paper and keep hot while frying the rest.

Braised Celery Hearts

Serves 4

One of the easiest vegetables to cook and one of the most delectable when freshly served. This dish has a concentrated flavour which can provide a foil to other gentler vegetables or is a good accompaniment to the full-bodied taste of game or roast beef.

4	celery hearts	4
30 g	butter	1 oz
	salt, pepper	

Wash and, if necessary, trim away any tired ends of celery stalk. If you are starting with whole heads of celery keep all the trimmings for soup.

Plunge the hearts into boiling salted water and simmer, covered, for 8–10 minutes.

Drain (keep the liquor for soup) and arrange the hearts in a single layer in a buttered casserole or lidded oven dish. Sprinkle with salt and pepper and dot with the rest of the butter.

Cover tightly and cook in a moderate oven, 180°C, 350°F, Gas Mark 4, for 25 minutes until tender and the butter has browned.

Thymed Potatoes

Serves 4

If the oven is on, it makes sense to cook potatoes alongside another dish. For this method try different herbs too, but dried thyme is available all year round, of course. The trick here is to use finely powdered dried thyme—available in France—or simply pulverise some in a coffee mill.

½ kg	waxy potatoes like Desirée	1 lb
	knob of butter	
½–1 teaspoon	powdered dried thyme	½–1 teaspoon
	salt, pepper	
4 tablespoons	top of milk	4 tablespoons

Peel the potatoes (or just scrub them if you prefer) and cut into 1 cm (½ in) dice. Butter an ovenproof dish generously. Put in layers of diced potatoes, sprinkle with thyme, salt and pepper now and again.

Dot with the rest of the butter and pour over the milk.

Cover and cook in a moderate oven, 180°C, 350°F, Gas Mark 4, for 30–40 minutes.

Stuffed Turnips in Cider

Serves 4

To me, the French seem to be real wizards with the turnip, a vegetable that in this country we appear to turn up our noses at. If you grow your own turnips, pull them from golf-ball to tennis-ball size (they are sweetest when small) and cook them whole.

4	young, tender turnips, tennis-ball size	4
1	thick slice wholemeal bread	1
60 g	smoked sausage or ham, diced	2 oz
6	green peppercorns, fresh or tinned, crushed	6
1 teaspoon	chopped parsley	1 teaspoon
2–3 tablespoons	single cream	2–3 tablespoons
	salt, pepper	
	knob of butter	
	a little cider	

Peel the turnips thinly or if very young simply scrub. Trim the tops and bases of each so that they will stand. Cut an X across the top and boil in salted water for 7–10 minutes until cooked enough to remove the centres.

Meanwhile turn the bread into breadcrumbs in a processor. Add the diced sausage or ham, the crushed peppercorns and chopped parsley and whizz for a second to mix. Bind with the cream and season with salt and pepper.

Holding a sharp knife vertical, trace a ring on the top of each turnip. Remove the flesh inside the ring with a teaspoon, chop finely, leaving a neat shell. Add the chopped turnip to the stuffing and spoon into the turnip shells, packing it down well. Place a small piece of butter on each.

Stand the turnips in an ovenproof dish. Pour the cider round and cover with a butter paper or piece of foil. Cook in a moderate oven, 180°C, 350°F, Gas Mark 4, for 20–30 minutes until the turnips are tender.

Potato Gnocchi with Tomato Sauce

Serves 4–5

A comforting Italian dish that is simple and relaxing to make. This recipe is from Marcella Hazan's inspiring *Classic Italian Cookbook*. Potato gnocchi are also very good with Pesto Sauce (see page 84) or just with unsalted butter, black pepper and freshly grated Parmesan cheese.

Tomato sauce:

1	onion, finely chopped	1
1–2	cloves garlic	1–2
2 tablespoons	olive oil	2 tablespoons
400 g	tinned Italian tomatoes, chopped	14 oz
½ teaspoon	sugar	½ teaspoon
½ teaspoon	chopped fresh basil or dried thyme	½ teaspoon
	salt, pepper	
¾ kg	old potatoes, preferably Desirée	1½ lb
135 g	plain flour	4½ oz

It is best to make this first and let it cook while you prepare the gnocchi.

Cook the onion and garlic in the olive oil until golden. Add the chopped tomatoes, sugar, basil or thyme, salt and pepper. Stir and when it comes to the boil, cover, lower heat and simmer gently for 30–40 minutes.

Scrub the potatoes and cook in boiling salted water. Drain and peel as soon as you can handle them. Push through a mouli-légumes on finest setting into a bowl.

Add almost all the flour and work in to make a smooth dough. Add the rest of the flour if the dough is still sticky. Divide the dough into three and roll out each piece on a floured board to make a long sausage as thick as your thumb.

Have ready a preserving pan with 5 litres (8 pints) of simmering salted water.

Cut the sausages into 18 mm (¾ in) lengths. Push each length against a floured 2-pronged fork, making a dent in the middle with your finger. Make all the gnocchi and then cook them in batches in the large pan of simmering water.

At first the gnocchi sink to the bottom of the pan. Once they've risen to the surface count for 8–10 seconds, then remove them with a slotted spoon to a hot gratin dish. Keep hot while you cook the rest.

Mash the tomato sauce with a fork and serve spooned over the gnocchi.

Hot Beetroot with Horseradish Cream

Serves 4

The flavour of hot beetroot is altogether more friendly than the cold, over-vinegared slices that are frequently the custom.

Even pickled beetroot is improved if you use a sweetened and spiced vinegar. But, in my opinion, beetroot is best treated as an excellent root vegetable in its own right.

500 g	freshly dug beetroot	1 lb
	a knob of butter	
	pepper, salt	
1–2 tablespoons	fresh horseradish root, grated	1–2 tablespoons
150 ml	soured cream	¼ pint
	chopped chervil or parsley	

Scrub the beetroot gently and cut off the leaves (if they are in good condition cook them like spinach as a green vegetable), but leave the roots intact.

Cover the beetroot with cold water, bring to the boil and cook gently, covered, on the hob or in a moderate oven until tender. Depending on size and age of the roots, this takes from 30–60 minutes.

Allow to cool a little in the water, then peel—the skin should be easy to remove.

Dice the beetroot into a buttered oven dish. Sprinkle with milled pepper and a little sea salt and cover with a buttered paper. Keep hot in a low oven.

Grate the horseradish into a bowl and mix in the soured cream. Spoon over the beetroot, sprinkle with chopped chervil or parsley and serve straight away.

Colcannon

In the tradition of hearty farmhouse food and none the worse for that. I am indebted to Elizabeth Craig's *Scottish Cookery Book* for making clear the lineage of champ—the large family of mashed potato dishes of which Colcannon is the cabbage version. In Scotland it is known as Rumbledethumps and if you replace the butter with cream the dish becomes Kailkenny.

500 g	boiled peeled potatoes	1 lb
500 g	boiled cabbage	1 lb
60 g	butter or dripping	2 oz
	salt, pepper	
	chopped parsley (optional)	
	chopped spring onions (optional)	

I prefer to make this dish with freshly cooked vegetables but they can be cooked ahead if you prefer, then fried to make a kind of Bubble and Squeak.

Sieve the potatoes and chop the cabbage. If the vegetables are hot, mix them together in a bowl and stir in the butter, salt, pepper, parsley and onions and serve piping hot.

If cold, melt the butter or dripping in a pan and add the potatoes mixed with the cabbage and other ingredients. Cook as a potato cake until brown underneath. Then turn over and brown the other side. Serve in wedges.

Glazed Jerusalem Artichokes with Walnuts

Serves 4

Root vegetables, braised in butter or pork dripping, intensify in flavour. Parsnips, tender turnips or swedes are all excellent this way.

500 g	Jerusalem artichokes	1 lb
60 g	butter or pork dripping	2 oz
	sliver of garlic (optional)	
45 g	walnuts or blanched hazelnuts, halved	1½ oz

Scrub the artichokes and bring to the boil in salted water. Simmer for 4–5 minutes or just long enough to be able to peel off the skin. If time is short peel the artichokes and blanch in boiling water for 2 minutes but you'll lose more of the vegetable in the peelings. Drain and cut into walnut sized pieces.

Melt the butter or dripping in a pan, stir the sliver of garlic around to give a hint of flavour, then remove and toss in the artichokes. Sauté the vegetables, shaking the pan now and again. When browned all over and nearly cooked add the nuts and cook for 1–2 minutes more.

Serve straight away with grilled or roast meat.

Spinach Moulds

Individual moulds lined with blanched spinach leaves are filled with a savoury mixture to make an agreeable separate course. Vary the fillings to fit whatever you have to hand.

¾ kg	fresh spinach	1½ lb
45 g	butter, melted	1½ oz
4 tablespoons	cooked rice	4 tablespoons
120 g	cooked ham or chicken, finely diced	4 oz
1 tablespoon	flaked almonds, toasted	1 tablespoon
1	large egg, beaten	1
	grated nutmeg or pepper	
300 ml	tomato sauce (see p. 113) or mushroom sauce (see p. 66)	½ pint

Sort through the spinach, discard the stems and set aside about 12 large leaves.

Rinse both piles of spinach. Steam or blanch the large leaves for 2–3 minutes and cool on a cloth. Cook the rest of the spinach for 5 minutes in the water clinging to the leaves. Drain well and chop finely.

Brush melted butter inside eight dariole moulds or four teacups and line with the whole spinach leaves, allowing some to come over the rim.

Mix the chopped spinach with the cooked rice, the rest of the melted butter, diced ham, almonds and the egg. Season with grated nutmeg or milled pepper.

Spoon the mixture into the lined moulds. Fold the spinach leaves over the top. Stand the moulds in a bain-marie and cook in a moderate oven, 180°C, 350°F, Gas Mark 4, for 30–40 minutes until the mixture is set.

Cool for 5 minutes then turn out on to a serving dish and spoon a little sauce over each mould.

Potato Latkes

Serves 4

Years ago, one of our children's favourite activities was to sit watching 'Blue Peter' with a large plate of potato latkes straight from the pan and a bottle of tomato ketchup to hand. In smaller amounts and with home-made chutney, I recommend them.

¾ kg	waxy potatoes, like Desirée	1½ lb
1	medium onion or clove of garlic	1
2 tablespoons	flour	2 tablespoons
2	eggs	2
	salt, pepper	
	caraway or dill seeds (optional)	
	oil for shallow frying	

Peel the potatoes and grate into a bowl. If you are not cooking the latkes straight away, cover the grated potato with cold water and a pinch of bicarbonate of soda. Drain and rinse the potatoes and pat dry before completing the dish.

Grate in the onion or garlic, add the flour and eggs, and mix thoroughly. Season with salt and pepper. Sometimes I add caraway or dill seeds to perk up the flavour.

Heat a thin layer of oil in a pan and fry tablespoons of the mixture until golden on both sides. Turn on to kitchen paper and serve very hot.

Red Cabbage with Apple and Onion

Serves 4–6

This is Katie Stewart's recipe for German style red cabbage from her *Times* column some years ago. One of the best ways with the vegetable, it goes well with winter eating, especially pork.

1	small red cabbage	1
	salt	
30 g	butter	1 oz
1	onion, peeled and chopped	1
2	large cooking apples, peeled and chopped	2
3 tablespoons	wine vinegar	3 tablespoons
30 g	caster sugar	1 oz

Discard any damaged outer leaves of the cabbage. Quarter and remove the stalk, then finely shred the rest and soak in cold water for 1 hour. (I have cooked the cabbage without soaking, but you may have to boil off some of the final liquid.)

Melt the butter in a large saucepan or cast enamelled casserole. Stir in the onion and cook until soft. Drain the cabbage and add to the pan with the apple. Mix everything together and pour in boiling water to a depth of 1 cm (½ in). Add the vinegar and sugar.

Cover tightly and bring to the boil. Simmer gently for 45 minutes on the hob or in a moderate oven, 180°C, 350°F, Gas Mark 4.

Marrow Stuffed with Souffléd Rice

Serves 4

Much to my husband's regret marrows grow easily in our garden. In defence, my marrows are simply courgettes that got away. Invariably cheap to buy, marrows are even free at some garden gates.

1 teacup	risotto or round grain rice	1 teacup
1 teacup	cold water	1 teacup
	bay leaf	
	slice of onion	
	salt, pepper	
1 medium	marrow	1 medium
2–3	rashers bacon, diced	2–3
30 g	butter	1 oz
2	spring onions, chopped	2
2	eggs, separated	2
2 tablespoons	Parmesan cheese, finely grated	2 tablespoons

Wash the rice thoroughly and bring to the boil in the cold water with the bay leaf, slice of onion and salt and pepper. Stir, cover tightly, turn down heat to lowest setting and cook for 17 minutes.

Meanwhile peel the marrow, unless the skin is very tender. Cut in half lengthways and cut away the centre with the seeds. Steam the marrow for 5–6 minutes.

Gently fry the bacon in the butter with the spring onions. Stir in the cooked rice and the egg yolks. Check the seasoning.

Arrange the marrow in a buttered oven dish. Spoon the rice into each half.

Whisk the egg whites until stiff. Fold in the cheese and spread over the rice. Bake in a moderate oven, 190°C, 375°F, Gas Mark 5, for 10 minutes and serve straight away.

Hungarian Lecsó with Noodles   *Serves 4–6*

As a sauce for noodles, pasta or meat, green and red peppers slow cooked until meltingly soft and aromatic are very good indeed. If you grow your own, and now that capsicums are grown here commercially and are excellent value, this is a splendid way of preparing them for freezing or bottling.

1 tablespoon	best pork dripping or sunflower oil	1 tablespoon
2	slices smoked streaky bacon, diced	2
1	large onion	1
2 teaspoons	sweet paprika	2 teaspoons
1 teaspoon	hot paprika	1 teaspoon
250 g	ripe tomatoes, peeled and sliced	8 oz
3	large green peppers, seeded and sliced	3
1	large red pepper, seeded and sliced	1
	salt	
250–350 g	noodles	8–12 oz

Heat the dripping or oil and cook the bacon until the fat runs. Add the onion and cook over moderate heat until clear and golden.

Stir in the two kinds of paprika and then the tomatoes. When the juice has started to run, pile in the peppers. Season with salt and stir.

Allow to cook gently, uncovered, for 30–40 minutes until of chutney consistency.

Cook the noodles in boiling salted water and serve on very hot dishes with lecsó spooned across them.

Variation: Lecsó with eggs
Turn the cooked lecsó into a shallow ovenproof dish. Use the back of a tablespoon to make depressions each large enough for an egg. Carefully break an egg into each space and season with salt and pepper.

Cover the dish with a hood of foil and bake in a moderate oven, 190°C, 375°F, Gas Mark 5, or steam, until the whites are just set.

Pan Haggerty

Serves 4

A Northumbrian version of the many European cheese and potato dishes. Add the smaller amount of cheese if serving the dish with meat.

½ kg	potatoes, peeled	1 lb
1 tablespoon	bacon fat	1 tablespoon
250 g	onions, thinly sliced	8 oz
60–120 g	cheese, Cheddar, Wensleydale or Cheshire, grated	2–4 oz

Thinly slice or grate the potatoes. Melt the bacon fat in a heavy based frying pan. Make a layer of potatoes, add a layer of onions and then some cheese. Repeat the layers, making sure to finish with potato.

Cover the pan and fry gently for 25–30 minutes, until the potatoes are cooked.

Brown the top by turning the whole cake over or pop under a hot grill. Turn the Pan Haggerty on to a plate and cut into wedges to serve.

Small Mushroom and Basil Tarts   *Serves 6*

This is a summer mushroom dish using the Italian combination of basil with mushrooms and well worth trying. Apparently most of us think of mushrooms as a winter vegetable, and consequently cultivated mushrooms are often very good value during the summer months.

Pâte brisée:

120 g	plain flour	4 oz
	good pinch of salt	
60 g	butter, slightly salted	2 oz
1	egg yolk	1
1–2 tablespoons	cold water	1–2 tablespoons

Filling:

180 g	button or small cap mushrooms	6 oz
2	spring onions, chopped	2
45 g	butter	1½ oz
1 tablespoon	flour	1 tablespoon
150 ml	creamy milk or single cream	¼ pint
	salt, pepper	
1 tablespoon	chopped fresh basil or use Pesto Sauce (p. 84)	1 tablespoon
	few leaves flat parsley to decorate	

Sieve the flour and salt into a bowl and rub in the butter. Mix to a dough with the egg yolk combined with the water. Wrap the pastry and chill for about 1 hour.

Roll out on a floured surface and line six small tartlet tins 10 cm (4 in) across. Prick the pastry bases and bake on a hot baking sheet in a moderately hot oven, 200°C, 400°F, Gas Mark 6, for about 10 minutes, until firm but not coloured.

Wipe the mushrooms and leave whole if button, otherwise quarter them. Cook gently with the spring onions in the melted butter. As soon as the mushrooms and onions are soft, lift out with a slotted spoon and divide between the pastry cases.

Sprinkle the flour into the pan and mix well over moderate heat. Gradually add the cream or milk and cook until thickened. Season with salt and pepper and stir in the basil or Pesto Sauce.

Spoon the sauce over the mushrooms and replace in the oven for 5–7 minutes, until the sauce bubbles. Serve hot straight away with a small piece of parsley placed on each.

Cauliflower with Soured Cream and Paprika Crumbs
Serves 4

These paprika crumbs are well worth making and freezing for garnishing other vegetables and cheese dishes. Here the contrast between the perfectly cooked cauliflower, the cool cream and the spicy breadcrumbs is very good indeed.

1	medium sized cauliflower	1
	salt	
30 g	butter	1 oz
1	clove garlic, finely chopped or crushed	1
1 teaspoon	hot paprika (or use sweet paprika and a speck of cayenne)	1 teaspoon
60 g	dry wholemeal breadcrumbs	2 oz
6 tablespoons	single cream	6 tablespoons
	juice of ½ lemon	

Trim the base and surplus leaves from the cauliflower and quarter. Place in a steamer and sprinkle with a little salt. Steam until just cooked but with still a hint of bite.

Meanwhile melt the butter in a pan and cook the garlic until golden. Stir in the paprika for 1 minute, then add the breadcrumbs. Fry them, stirring all the time until crisp and golden red. Keep hot.

Add the lemon juice to the cream and stir until thick.

Arrange the cauliflower on a hot serving dish, spoon over the cream and sprinkle with the crumbs. Serve at once.

MEAT

From numerous discussions with people of all ages I find that above all others, meat is the ingredient that causes the most anxiety to those trying to eat well at low cost. Certainly meat can make the biggest hole in your purse. It is perhaps no surprise that it is in this area of eating that misconceptions proliferate.

First of all, I consider that we need to escape the tyranny of thinking that only roast and grilled meat represent the pinnacle of good eating. This medieval attitude dates from the time when the roasting spit was supreme in the kitchen. Unfortunately this method of cooking is not only the most expensive, it is the least imaginative. Consequently the most popular dish in restaurants in Britain today is grilled steak—a dish so easily, and more cheaply, prepared at home. Whenever I eat in a restaurant I choose food either made with ingredients that I myself can't come by easily or fresh food that has been prepared with a high degree of skill and flair. Not enough people agree, sad to say, so that the menus of most restaurants and hotels reflect, simply, expensive fast food, or worse, dishes that travel from freezer to micro-wave while you linger over your first course. I welcome the day when menus must reveal all, or the restauranteur is secure enough to allow us to enter through the kitchens. Unfortunately there is still a deep-rooted suspicion in our country, probably dating from the Norman Conquest, of any food that is not immediately recognisable as a leg of this or a breast of that. Any dish, and especially meat, from sweetbreads to a suprême of chicken, bathed in sauce or well seasoned and imaginatively served, is frequently regarded as 'mucked up' or, worse, possibly foreign in influence.

The British style of butchering is not always an asset to budget gourmets. We are frequently sold unnecessary and unwelcome fat with our meat which in France and Germany finds its way into delicious cured meats and sausages of which we are so lamentably short. I once spent an instructive day in the Nahe valley with two German friends, helping with the disposal of a freshly killed pig. It was early one misty October morning when we met the local butcher in his spotlessly clean slaughterhouse. And it was fascinating to discover how every particle of pig was prepared for human consumption.

Handsome, well-trimmed joints of leg and loin were cut to a variety of sizes for the freezer. Every drop of blood was kept for Blutwurst and the equivalent of our black puddings. Some meat was brined to be later canned or preserved in jars. Any offal not destined for the freezer went with plenty of pork fat into a giant mincer to be turned into a variety of wursts and salamis, each kind prepared to a much-treasured recipe. After filling the casings, some sausages were cooked straight away in a large cauldron, while others were intended for smoking along with the brined ham. Not even the tail or snout was left—just a pail of bones which were going to be boiled later.

We started at 7 a.m. and left after scrubbing out the place in mid-afternoon, having been revived from time to time by coffee and Kirschwasser. The village butcher, two German housewives and myself had disposed of the pig, which, in a day, provided enough meat and sausages for two families for six months. No part of the animal was regarded as less deserving of serious attention than any other and no large lorry from a petfood firm collected material which seems to faze us. Whatever did family pets eat a hundred years ago? The whole episode was a splendid example of self-help for budget gourmets, and some hard-working farmers' wives and smallholders, here, perform similar miracles with their meat.

In the past many more butchers did so too. Finding a butcher who even makes his own sausages is a treat these days. Frequently I resort to making my own and I include the recipe. If you are interested in dealing with your own butchering, especially the cottager's favourite animal, the pig, there are two invaluable handbooks. Jane Grigson's classic, *Charcuterie and French Pork Cookery* and *The Book of the Sausage* by Antony and Araminta Coxe.

I like to get the most out of any expensive-to-produce animal protein that I buy. On the whole, it is better to buy as large a piece of meat as you can afford, since the meat will shrink less and taste more succulent. My butcher offers an inducement by lowering the price per lb if you buy, for example, a whole leg of lamb rather than a half. This is fine if there are lots of mouths to feed or you can afford the outlay. If not, think about getting together with a few friends to divide too large a piece of meat. But apart from throwing a party, I suggest cutting the meat into smaller pieces and cooking each differently.

I am sure you've noticed that the larger the chicken the less price per kilo or pound and, of course, the greater proportion of flesh to bone. I try to buy a large roasting bird and then set about tackling it in a variety of ways. I first of all remove all the breast meat, in two large pieces which can be cooked whole, batted out thin and rolled around a stuffing or they can be cooked as escalopes. Or this breast meat can be used for Spring Vegetable Terrine, Chicken Kiev or Stir-Fried Vegetables with Chicken. The legs or wings could be detached for cooking with spices, in orange juice or wine, although I prefer to poach the breastless bird with vegetables and herbs. Then the legs and wings are eaten hot or cold with a delicate sauce, perhaps lemon or a cream sauce, using some of the stock. All the remaining meat goes into a salad or pilaff, and the rest of the poaching stock and giblets into soups and sauces during the next few days. Any meat or stock not required at the time is frozen until needed.

Don't always accept the doctrine that meat which requires hours of cooking is bound to be cheaper. Look critically at your circumstances. If you cook on a continuous burning stove, then you are able to use the whole repertoire of traditional slow cooked recipes. But if you use bottled gas or have a metered electricity supply, fuel may be a major cost in your food preparation.

There is one cooking ingredient above all others which will elevate your meat cooking to a new degree of deliciousness, and it has the advantage of saving cooking time by tenderising your meat at the same time. It is wine: red or white. Perfectly acceptable and drinkable wines can be bought for under £2 a bottle through wine clubs, on offer in wine merchants and supermarkets. My local wine merchant frequently has bin-end offers and also sells unlabelled and presumably blended wine very cheaply indeed. It is a great deal better than the plonk we used to drink as students. I agree with Paul Levy of the *Observer* that there is no such thing as 'cooking wine'; there are just good, bad and middling wines. My point is that a middling wine, on price and taste, is excellent for using when cooking meat. As a marinade for tougher or more dense cuts of meat wine is without equal. (A recipe for marinade is given in Chapter 6, p. 168.) But it is also worth remembering that cider can be used instead, or as an alternative a small amount of lemon or lime juice can be used to good effect.

As an ingredient in a sauce—even just a dash—wine gives a new and welcome dimension to many dishes.

I hope that in the recipes that follow you will find some meat dishes that you like and that will free you from the minced meat merry-go-round that occupies so much space in some budget cook books.

Noisettes of Lamb with Nut Stuffing

Serves 4

Boned lamb cutlets are rounded out with an apricot and peanut stuffing that complements the meat.

120 g	best dried apricots	4 oz
150 ml	warm water	¼ pint
4	lamb cutlets	4
1	thick slice wholemeal bread	1
75 g	salted roasted peanuts	2½ oz
¼ teaspoon	ground mace	¼ teaspoon
	salt, pepper	
2	sweet oranges	2

Gently cook the apricots in the warm water for 15–20 minutes until soft and almost all the water has been absorbed.

Use a short sharp knife to cut away the bone from each cutlet and remove all surplus fat. Break the bread into pieces into a processor or blender. Add the nuts and chop both together until fine but still crunchy. Turn into a bowl and add the mace, some salt and pepper and the grated rind of one orange.

Chop the apricots in the processor and add to the breadcrumbs. Mix the stuffing with the juice of one orange until it adheres.

Divide the stuffing between the four boned cutlets and tuck the meat around the stuffing neatly. Secure with butcher's twine.

Cook the meat in a buttered flameproof dish in a moderate oven, 180°C, 350°F, Gas Mark 4, for 35–45 minutes until cooked.

Transfer the meat to a hot serving dish. Pour off all the surplus fat and grate the rind from the other orange and its juice into the pan. If not very juicy add a little extra juice. Bubble over moderate heat for 2–3 minutes. Pour a little sauce over each noisette and serve.

Pork Marinated in Cider

Local cider and apples offset the richness of the meat, and enhance the flavour.

¾ kg	shoulder of pork, sliced	1½ lb
	salt, pepper	
	few sprigs or leaves fresh thyme	
	and sage	
	or	
½ teaspoon	dried thyme and sage	½ teaspoon
1	onion	1
1	carrot	1
300 ml	dry cider	½ pint
2 tablespoons	butter	2 tablespoons
½ teaspoon	tomato purée	½ teaspoon
2 teaspoons	honey	2 teaspoons
3 or 4	eating apples, Cox's orange pippin	3 or 4

Arrange the sliced meat in a single layer in a shallow ovenproof dish and season with salt and freshly ground black pepper. Remove the leaves from the thyme and chop the sage and sprinkle on top.

Slice the onion and carrot and arrange over the meat. Pour over the cider and set the dish aside in a cool place to marinate for 8–12 hours.

Lift out the meat and pat dry on kitchen paper. Pour the marinade and vegetables into a jug.

Melt the butter in a pan and quickly sear the meat on both sides. Warm the oven dish, replace the meat in it and keep hot. Pour the marinade into the buttery pan and add the tomato purée and honey. Bring to the boil and simmer for 4 minutes.

Meanwhile wipe and core the apples and cut into fairly thick slices. Arrange the slices over the meat and pour over the contents of the pan.

Cover the oven dish with buttered paper or foil and cook in a moderate oven, 190°C, 375°F, Gas Mark 5, for 45–60 minutes. Remove the covering for the last 10 minutes of cooking time to brown the apples a little.

Navarin of Lamb

This fine lamb dish can be prepared in winter with appropriate vegetables or, even better, in spring—Navarin Printanier—with new potatoes, tender turnips, baby carrots, finger-sized French beans and possibly new peas. If you use new season's lamb it makes a truly memorable meal.

2 kg	shoulder of lamb	4 lb
30–60 g	butter	1–2 oz
1 tablespoon	white sugar	1 tablespoon
300 ml	stock or water	½ pint
350 g	tomatoes, peeled and chopped	12 oz
1	clove garlic, crushed	1
	salt, pepper	
1 tablespoon	flour	1 tablespoon
	bouquet of thyme and rosemary	
	bay leaf	
500 g	small new potatoes	1 lb
500 g	small turnips	1 lb
250 g	baby onions or spring onions	8 oz
180 g	young French beans	6 oz
120 g	shelled new peas	4 oz

With a very sharp knife cut the meat from the shoulder of lamb, discarding all skin, bone and fat. Cut the meat in 2½–5 cm (1–2 in) pieces.

Melt the butter in a pan and sear the meat quickly in batches. Transfer the meat to a hot casserole. Add the sugar to the remaining butter in the pan and allow it to caramelise to give a good colour to the dish.

Pour the stock and tomatoes into the pan and stir until all the sugar and pan juices have been dissolved. Add the garlic. Season the meat with salt and pepper and sprinkle the flour over, then pour over the liquid from the pan. Bury the bouquet garni and the bay leaf in the casserole.

Cover and cook in a moderate oven, 190°C, 375°F, Gas Mark 5, for 1 hour.

Meanwhile cook the potatoes, turnips and onions separately in salted water for 3 minutes. Add to the casserole and cook for a further 20 minutes. Cook the beans and peas, drain and spoon over the meat. Coat the vegetables with the sauce and serve piping hot.

Greek-style Meat Balls with Lemon and Mint
Serves 4

An excellent summer dish. It is simple enough to mince veal or pork at home if your butcher does not supply it. Use a grinding disc with 4 mm (⅛ inch) holes.

500 g	minced veal or lean pork	1 lb
	salt, pepper	
1	large lemon	1
	handful of mint leaves, finely chopped	
1	egg yolk	1
1 tablespoon	seasoned flour	1 tablespoon
	a little oil, preferably olive, for frying	
1 tablespoon	pine nuts	1 tablespoon

Mix the minced meat with some salt and pepper and the finely grated rind of the lemon and about two-thirds of the chopped mint. Bind together with the egg yolk.

Take teaspoons of the mixture, dip one hand in the seasoned flour and shape the meat into small neat balls. I usually make about 24.

Fry the meat balls in the hot oil in a shallow pan; shake it frequently to keep the meat balls turning over and well shaped. Fry until golden on all sides and cooked through.

Add the pine nuts and sprinkle over the remainder of the mint. Pour in the juice of the lemon. Simmer for 2 minutes then serve straight away with plain boiled rice.

This dish is also good served cold with a rice salad.

Stir-fried Chicken and Vegetables

Serves 3–4

Chinese stir-frying has enlivened our cuisine during the last few years. I prefer to use a wok but a capacious frying pan will do. It takes longer to cut up the ingredients than to cook them (it is an enjoyable task to chat over, if there is no hurry) but the slicing disc on a processor can help with root vegetables. Because nothing is overcooked, this dish is surprisingly filling, and is an excellent way of feeding four people with two breasts of chicken.

2	breasts of chicken	2
5 cm	piece of fresh ginger	2 in
1	clove garlic	1
1	large carrot, shredded	1
	piece of celeriac or tender turnip, thinly sliced	
	few spring onions, cut in lengths	
	few French beans or courgettes, cut in short pieces	
1–2 tablespoons	sunflower or sesame oil	1–2 tablespoons
1–2	tomatoes, chopped	1–2
	handful of bean sprouts	
	soy sauce	

Cut the chicken into narrow strips. Peel and finely shred the ginger into matchsticks, chop the garlic.

Prepare all the rest of the vegetables and arrange in small heaps on your chopping board so that they can be added to the wok in order, the root vegetables taking longer to cook than the fleshier ones.

Heat the oil in the wok or pan until really hot and about to smoke. Add the ginger and garlic and stir for a few moments until changing colour. Add the chicken and fry, stirring all the time until all trace of pink has disappeared. Use a slotted spoon to remove the meat to a hot dish and add the vegetables a few at a time so that the temperature remains high. Cook the root vegetables first, adding the spring onions, tomatoes and bean sprouts last.

Cook very quickly for just 2–3 minutes, ensuring that the vegetables still retain some crispness.

Return the chicken to the wok and sprinkle with soy sauce. Stir well and serve straight away with boiled rice.

Gammon Steaks with Apricots   *Serves 4*

Thick slices of bacon or ham which have very little waste are
often to be had at bargain prices. My butcher sells them in
pairs and many supermarkets pack them individually, making
them an ideal meal for one.

4	slices of gammon or green bacon	4
400 g	tin of apricot halves in juice	14 oz
30 g	butter	1 oz
1	small onion, finely chopped	1
1	stick of celery, diced	1
1 tablespoon	flour	1 tablespoon
	a little stock or water	
	splash Madeira or dry sherry	

Cut off any rind from the gammon and snip the fat 2 or 3
times to encourage the meat to stay flat while cooking. Place
the meat in a buttered ovenproof dish and pour over half
the juice from the tin of apricots. Grill or bake the meat in
a moderate oven, 190°C, 375°F, Gas Mark 5, for 15–20
minutes, turning the meat over halfway through.

Then make the sauce. Melt the butter in a pan and cook the
onion and celery until soft. Stir in the flour and then the
cooking juices from the gammon. Add a little stock or water, if
necessary, to make a thin sauce, plus a splash of Madeira or
dry sherry. Leave the sauce to bubble very gently.

Arrange the drained apricot halves over the meat and
return to the grill or oven to heat through. Pour the sauce over
and serve.

Green Rice Rings filled with Turkey in Cream Sauce and Cranberries *Serves 8*

This dish tastes and looks good—it is one of the most popular that I have ever devised.

350 g	Patna rice	12 oz
½ litre	water	¾ pint
1 tablespoon	butter	1 tablespoon
	salt, pepper	
250 g	cooked spinach	8 oz
60 g	butter, melted	2 oz
	grated nutmeg	
¾ kg	breast of turkey	1½ lb
1	small onion, sliced	1
1	carrot, sliced	1
1	stick of celery, sliced	1
2	bay leaves	2
4	cloves	4
1 tablespoon	each of butter and flour blended together to make beurre manié	1 tablespoon
250 g	fresh cranberries	8 oz
	rind and juice of 1 orange	
100 g	sugar	3½ oz
150 ml	single cream	¼ pint

Wash the rice carefully in a sieve under cold running water until the water runs clear (4–5 minutes). Turn the rice into a saucepan with the water, butter, salt and pepper. Bring to the boil, stir and turn down the heat to the lowest setting. Cover with a tight-fitting lid and cook for 17 minutes.

Meanwhile purée the spinach with the melted butter and season with nutmeg. Mix the spinach into the cooked rice and stir to distribute evenly. Pack into eight buttered ring moulds, pressing down fairly firmly as you do so. Set the moulds on a baking sheet and cover with a sheet of buttered foil. Set aside until needed.

Gently poach the breasts of turkey in just enough water to cover together with the onion, carrot, celery, bay leaves and cloves, plus some salt and pepper. When just cooked, remove the meat and cut into thin slices. Strain the liquor back into the pan and reduce over high heat until it measures 300 ml (½ pint). Blend the butter with the flour to make beurre manié, divide into small pieces and gradually add to the turkey stock, stirring until thickened. Cover the sauce and allow to cook gently, preferably over simmering water, for 30 minutes until all trace of flouriness has disappeared.

Cook the cranberries with the rind and juice of the orange until the cranberries begin to 'pop'. Remove from the heat, stir in the sugar, cover and keep warm.

Reheat the rice in a moderate oven, 180°C, 350°F, Gas Mark 4, for 15–20 minutes. Stir the cream into the sauce, add the sliced turkey and reheat gently but do not boil.

To serve, turn the rice rings out on to individual plates, spoon the turkey in sauce into the centre of each and top with a tablespoon of cranberries.

Beef Curry

The satisfaction of blending and grinding your own curry powder is only outweighed by the taste of the final dish. Below I give one of my blends, but the proportions are infinitely variable. If you like curry, you will soon work out your own blends, with different characteristics: perhaps a little hotter or less so, maybe more cinnamon or cumin. Most curries benefit from being made 1–2 days ahead, and reheated to serve. This makes them ideal for parties.

Home-made curry powder:

	Parts (to start with make 1 teaspoon = 1 part)
black peppercorns	1
dried red chilli	1 pod
cloves, whole	1
cinnamon	½ stick
cardamom pods	1
coriander seed	6
cumin seed	2
fenugreek seed	½

Curry:

1 kg	shin of beef or other stewing cut	2 lb
2 tablespoons	ghee, oil or dripping	2 tablespoons
1–2	onions, chopped	1–2
1–2	cloves garlic, chopped	1–2
2 tablespoons	home-ground curry powder	2 tablespoons
½–1 teaspoon	ground turmeric	½–1 teaspoon
1–2 teaspoons	salt	1–2 teaspoons
1 tablespoon	fresh ginger root, grated	1 tablespoon
400 g	tinned Italian tomatoes	14 oz
1 tablespoon	marmalade, sharp jelly, or brown sugar	1 tablespoon

Measure the spices into a bowl, break up the cinnamon stick and discard the pods of the cardamom seed. Tip everything into a clean coffee mill and grind to a fine powder.

Trim the meat of skin and any fat and cut into neat pieces about 4 cm (1½ in) in size.

Heat the ghee, oil or dripping in a casserole or saucepan and cook the onions and garlic until soft and transparent.

Stir in the curry powder and turmeric and cook for 1–2 minutes.

Add the meat and stir to coat with the spice mixture. Stir in the salt, ginger, tomatoes and marmalade. Bring to the boil.

Cover tightly and cook in a slow oven, 160°C, 325°F, Gas Mark 3, for about 3 hours or until tender, or cook over low heat on top of the stove.

Serve the curry with dhal, boiled rice and a selection of Indian pickles and chutneys.

Honey Glazed Lamb with Pineapple and Green Pepper

Serves 4

A good pick-me-up for slow-thawed New Zealand lamb chops.

4	chump lamb chops	4
	knob of butter	
1 tablespoon	set honey	1 tablespoon
1 teaspoon	Dijon mustard	1 teaspoon
¼ teaspoon	ground ginger	¼ teaspoon
¼ teaspoon	ground fenugreek	¼ teaspoon
1	small green pepper	1
4	pineapple rings	4

Trim any surplus fat from the chops and place them in a buttered fireproof dish.

Mix the honey, mustard, ginger and fenugreek to a smooth paste. Spread two-thirds of the mixture over the chops—they can now be left for up to 2 hours or can be cooked straight away.

Grill the chops under high heat for about 10 minutes. Turn them over and spread the rest of the honey glaze on the other side. Grill for a further 5 minutes.

Meanwhile seed and dice the green pepper and cut the pineapple into chunks. Sprinkle them over and around the meat and grill for about 10 minutes or until the meat is cooked to your liking, and baste with the sauce now and again. Serve with rice or potatoes.

Spatchcock Chicken

Serves 4

Spatchcock comes from 'dispatch cock', meaning a quickly killed and cooked chicken and dates from the sixteenth century. By the simple device of cutting through the chicken to make a single layer, the cooking time is much reduced.

2 × 1 kg	roasting chicken	2 × 2–3 lb
	juice of ½ lemon	
	salt, pepper	
60 g	butter, melted	2 oz
1 tablespoon	mustard powder	1 tablespoon
	a little milk	
2 tablespoons	dry breadcrumbs	2 tablespoons
	watercress, to garnish	

Prepare the chicken by cutting through the backbone with poultry shears. Flatten each bird with the blade of a knife and secure the legs with a wooden skewer.

Brush the skin with lemon juice and sprinkle with salt and pepper. Set the grill on high. Arrange the chicken in a buttered roasting tin and brush with the melted butter.

Grill the chicken on both sides, basting with butter now and again, until the meat is cooked. This usually takes about 20 minutes altogether but make sure the chicken is not under-cooked.

Brush the skin side of the chicken with the mustard mixed with the milk and dust with breadcrumbs. Grill for a few minutes more until the breadcrumbs are golden and crisp.

Serve garnished with watercress and potato croquettes (see p. 109).

Provençal Beef

Shin of beef, tenderised by marinading, makes this cheap and delicious dish which reheats splendidly.

¾ kg	shin of beef, cut in slices	1½ lb
300 ml	cheap red wine, preferably Côtes du Rhône	½ pint
1–2	cloves garlic, crushed bouquet of thyme and rosemary *or*	1–2
1 teaspoon	dried herbes de Provence salt, pepper	1 teaspoon
2–3 tablespoons	olive oil	2–3 tablespoons
400 g	tinned Italian tomatoes	14 oz
24	black olives	24
180 g	button mushrooms, quartered	6 oz
1 teaspoon each	butter and flour, blended together to make beurre manié chopped parsley	1 teaspoon

Cut the meat into 5 cm (2 in) chunks, discarding any skin and gristle, but leave the marbling in the meat which will contribute to the flavour.

In a bowl mix the wine with the garlic, herbs, some salt and pepper. Add the meat, turning it over in the marinade. Cover the bowl tightly and chill in the refrigerator for 24 hours.

Remove the meat from the marinade with a slotted spoon and drain well.

Heat the oil in the base of a flameproof casserole and quickly sear the meat, in 2 or 3 batches, if necessary. Add the marinade and tomatoes and bring to the boil. Cover tightly and cook in a slow oven, 160°C, 325°F, Gas Mark 3, for 2–2½ hours. Add the olives and cook for a further 45 minutes. Stir in the mushrooms and cook for 15 minutes.

If the sauce is still thin at this stage, thicken with the beurre manié added in small pieces and cooked over moderate heat until thickened.

Serve the dish sprinkled with chopped parsley, accompanied by plain boiled rice or noodles.

Butterflied Lamb with Yoghurt and Ginger

Serves 8–12

A boned leg of lamb, said to resemble a butterfly in shape, tastes even better after marinating in yoghurt with fresh ginger. Far quicker to cook than the traditional roast, a leg of lamb this way feeds more people, due to the lack of shrinkage. I recommend this dish for a party served, in slices, hot or cold.

2–3 kg	leg of lamb	4–6 lb
300 ml	natural yoghurt	½ pint
5 cm	piece of fresh ginger	2 ins
1	clove garlic, crushed	1
	salt	
	good pinch cayenne pepper	

Using a small sharp knife, follow the line of the bone down through the leg of lamb cutting away the meat in short even strokes. The bone should come away remarkably cleanly and the meat may or may not resemble a butterfly. Bat the meat out a little until it is of even thickness, about 5 cm (2 in) all over.

Measure the yoghurt into a bowl and grate the ginger into it. (I don't bother to peel the ginger, but I do discard the fibrous part of the ginger left behind by the grater.) Mix in the crushed clove of garlic and some salt and cayenne pepper.

Spread the meat, skin side down, on a grid in a roasting tin. Spoon the marinade over the surface of the meat, brushing it well into the crevices. Leave, covered, for 4–8 hours at room temperature.

Cook the meat in a hot oven, 200°C, 400°F, Gas Mark 6, for about 30 minutes until cooked but still pink in the centre and with the marinade starting to brown in an appetising way

Cut into thin slices across the meat for serving.

Half a leg of lamb can also be cooked this way.

Blanquette de Veau

Serves 4

Now that veal is more widely available, you can often pick up a bargain if the pieces are uneven. These, or the shoulder, are excellent for this classic dish that Madame Maigret makes so often.

¾ kg	shoulder or pie veal	1½ lb
1	carrot, leek and stick of celery, sliced	1
	bouquet garni of parsley stalks, thyme and bay leaf	
	juice of ½ lemon	
	salt, pepper	
12	small pickling onions	12
250 g	button mushrooms	8 oz
45 g	butter	1½ oz
45 g	flour	1½ oz
⅛ teaspoon	ground mace	⅛ teaspoon
2	egg yolks	2
4 tablespoons	single cream or top of milk	4 tablespoons

Cut the veal into 4 cm (1½ in) cubes and soak in cold water for 1 hour. Drain and cover with fresh water, in a pan, with the onion, carrot, leek, celery and bouquet garni. Season with lemon juice and salt and pepper. Bring to the boil and skim until all the froth has gone.

Cover the pan and simmer gently on top of the stove or in a slow oven, 160°C, 325°F, Gas Mark 3, for 1 hour.

Add the small onions and mushrooms and cook for a further 30 minutes or until the meat is tender.

Strain the liquid from the meat and reduce over high heat until it measures 600 ml (1 pint). Arrange the meat and vegetables in a serving dish and keep hot.

Melt the butter in a pan, stir in the flour off the heat, then cook for 1–2 minutes. Gradually whisk in the reduced stock and cook until thickened. Season with mace.

Mix the egg yolks with the cream or top of milk and add to the sauce, cook until thickened but do not let it boil.

Pour the sauce over the meat and vegetables and keep hot until ready to serve.

Lamb Cutlets in Pastry Ribbons   *Serves 4*

I devised this recipe for those who eat alone. It is simple to prepare just one cutlet, or several, and freeze the rest. The meat is flavoured with a mixture from ancient Rome, said to have been popular with supposedly abstemious ladies who needed to sweeten their breath.

4	lean lamb cutlets	4
1 tablespoon	clear honey	1 tablespoon
2 tablespoons	fresh mint, finely chopped	2 tablespoons
350 g	puff pastry, fresh or frozen	12 oz
	egg yolk for glazing	

Use a short sharp knife to cut the bone out of each cutlet. Trim away any surplus fat.

Mix the honey with the mint and brush the meat all over.

Roll out the pastry to 3 mm (⅛ in) thickness. Cut strips 2½ cms (1 in) wide from the pastry.

Wrap the pastry ribbons around each cutlet, slightly over-lapping, until the meat is covered.

Place the meat parcels on a dampened baking sheet and brush with egg yolk.

Cook in a moderately hot oven, 200°C, 400°F, Gas Mark 6, for 30–40 minutes, depending on size, until the meat is cooked and the pastry is golden and puffy.

Stuffed Cabbage Leaves

Serves 4

An improving way with a Savoy cabbage.

180 g	minced veal or pork	6 oz
4 rashers	smoked streaky bacon, diced	4 rashers
120 g	white breadcrumbs	4 oz
1	small onion, minced	1
½ teaspoon	oregano or marjoram	½ teaspoon
1 teaspoon	grated lemon rind	1 teaspoon
	salt, pepper	
2	eggs, beaten	2
8–12	large cabbage leaves, preferably Savoy	8–12
300 ml	chicken or veal stock	½ pint

In a bowl mix the veal or pork with the bacon, breadcrumbs, onion and oregano or marjoram. Stir in the lemon rind, salt and pepper and mix to a firm consistency with the beaten eggs.

Wash the cabbage leaves well, then blanch in salted boiling water for 1–2 minutes. Drain and refresh in cold water.

Take each leaf and with the stalk side towards you, place 1 heaped tablespoon of stuffing in the middle of the leaf. Fold each side over the stuffing, then from the stalk side roll up the leaf.

Arrange the stuffed leaves, flaps down, in one layer in a lidded ovenproof dish. Pour over the stock and cover. Cook in a moderate oven, 190°C, 375°F, Gas Mark 5, for 40 minutes. Serve with a hot tomato sauce (see p. 113).

Chicken Kiev

I remember eating the most delicious Chicken Kiev ever in a small railway hotel in Yugoslavia. But in fact this is simple enough to make at home. As you cut into the crisp outside hot, flavoured butter spurts out over the tender meat.

Garlic butter:

60 g	unsalted butter	2 oz
2 teaspoons	lemon juice	2 teaspoons
1	clove garlic, crushed	1
1 tablespoon	finely chopped parsley	1 tablespoon
	salt, pepper	
4	suprêmes or breasts of chicken	4
	seasoned flour	
1	egg, beaten	1
	dry white breadcrumbs	
	fat for deep frying	

Soften the butter and beat in the lemon juice and garlic. Work in the chopped parsley and season with salt and pepper to taste. Spoon the butter on to a piece of greaseproof paper and chill until firm. Divide into 4 fingers and freeze.

Skin the chicken, then cut a pocket in the meat. Place a finger of garlic butter in the pocket and then roll up the meat carefully to enclose the butter securely.

Dip each piece of chicken in the flour, the egg and then the breadcrumbs, patting them in well.

Chill for 2 hours.

To cook, heat the fat to 180°C, 350°F, Gas Mark 4, and deep-fry the chicken, two at a time, for 6–8 minutes until golden brown. Drain on kitchen paper and keep hot while you cook the rest.

Pot Roast Chicken with Oranges and Mint

Serves 6–8

A good recipe for early summer when fresh mint is first available again.

2–3 kg	fresh roasting chicken, including giblets	4–6 lb
4	sweet oranges	4
	knob of butter	
300 ml	orange juice	½ pint
1	slice of onion	1
1	stick of celery, chopped	1
1	carrot, chopped	1
1	bouquet garni	1
	salt, few peppercorns	
8 sprigs	fresh mint	8
1 teaspoon	each of butter and flour blended together to make beurre manié	1 teaspoon

Remove the giblets from the chicken. Cut two oranges into quarters and stuff into the body of the chicken. Grind some pepper and salt over the chicken and place in a buttered casserole.

Pour the orange juice around the bird and arrange a sliced orange over the breast. Cover tightly and cook in a moderate oven, 190°C, 375°F, Gas Mark 5, for 1½–2 hours, depending on the size of the chicken. The chicken is cooked when there is no trace of blood at the leg joint.

Place the giblets in a casserole in water to cover, with the onion, celery, carrot and bouquet garni plus a little salt and the peppercorns. Cook, covered, in the oven at the same time as the chicken for about 1 hour.

Strain the liquor from the giblets and reduce over high heat to about 150 ml (¼ pint).

Pour the orange liquor from the chicken into a pan and remove any excess fat with a sheet of kitchen paper laid over the surface. Keep the chicken hot in the covered casserole.

Chop half the mint leaves and simmer in the orange sauce for 2–3 minutes. Add the finely grated rind and juice of the remaining orange and the reduced giblet stock. Bring to the boil and thicken the sauce with the beurre manié, added in pea-sized pieces.

Transfer the chicken to a hot serving plate (joint or carve it if you wish). Pour a little sauce round the chicken, arrange the sprigs of mint on top and serve the rest of the sauce separately.

Boeuf à la Mode

Serves 10–12

At first sight this might look a somewhat extravagant dish on time and ingredients. However it has the advantage of being served hot the first day and cold another. Each in their own way delicious, serving the beef cold in its jelly wins for flavour and certainly feeds more. Sometimes, as a compromise, I serve a little of the liquor as a soup and leave everything else to serve chilled. If you wish, marinate the beef in the wine with the herbs overnight first.

2 kg	top rump or topside of beef	4 lb
	salt, pepper	
	knob of butter	
4	slices smoked streaky bacon, cut into strips	4
2	onions, sliced	2
	small glass of brandy (optional)	
300 ml	red or dry white wine, ideally Burgundy	½ pint
2	calf's or pig's feet, split and washed	2
¾ kg	carrots	1½ lb
2	sticks celery, chopped	2
1 or 2	cloves garlic, halved	1 or 2
6	peppercorns	6
	bouquet of fresh herbs, tied with a strip of orange peel	
up to 1 litre	light beef stock or water	1–2 pints

To serve cold:

180 g	baby or pickling onions	6 oz
180 g	young green beans	6 oz
2–3	tender turnips	2–3

If your butcher is preparing the meat ask him to bard it with pork rather than beef fat. In any case, if you can, add extra fat by threading small strips, lardons, of firm pork fat into the beef to further improve the flavour and consistency. Season the meat by rubbing salt and milled pepper into it.

Melt the butter in a heavy cast iron casserole with a tight

155

fitting lid and cook the bacon and onions until starting to change colour. Remove the bacon and onions and brown the meat all over. If including it, add the warmed brandy and flame it. Pour in the wine and allow to bubble a little. Wedge the split and washed calf's or pig's feet one each side of the meat. Return the bacon and onions to the casserole and add a third of the carrots, the celery, garlic, peppercorns and herbs with a little more salt. Pour in enough stock or water to just cover the meat.

Cover and cook very slowly indeed for 3½–5 hours: on the hob set to low, or in a slow oven, 150°C, 300°F, Gas Mark 2. If you have a fan oven you may need an even lower temperature. After 3 hours check that the level of the liquid has not dropped and make up if necessary. Cook further until a skewer goes into the meat easily.

To serve hot, slice some of the meat from the narrow end and serve with the vegetables removed with a slotted spoon and the rest of the carrots, cooked separately.

To serve cold in jelly, allow the meat to cool in the liquid. Then remove the meat and discard all the fat, except the lardons. Take out the calf's feet and dice the meaty parts; if desired they can be breadcrumbed and grilled for eating later. Strain everything else into a jug and chill until the fat has set on top and can be removed. You can judge the quality of the set now—if necessary in hot weather add a little dissolved gelatine to assist it.

Cook the rest of the carrots, and the baby onions, beans and turnips cut into ovals.

Now arrange a layer of carrots, onions, beans and turnips on the base of a terrine. Heat the jelly to liquify, pour over some and chill to set. Slice the beef and reassemble it on the set jelly and pour more jelly around it. Chill until firm, then arrange the rest of the vegetables on top and finish with the remainder of the jelly. Chill well, turn out and slice where the meat is cut. Serve with a salad.

Chicken cooked in Coconut Milk

Serves 4–6

A delicately spiced chicken dish, perfect for summer eating. This is my slight adaptation of Rosemary Hume's recipe.

250 g	fresh grated coconut	8 oz
	or	
90 g	desiccated coconut	3 oz
¾ litre	boiling water	1¼ pints
½ teaspoon	black peppercorns	½ teaspoon
1 teaspoon	coriander seeds	1 teaspoon
⅛ teaspoon	cayenne pepper	⅛ teaspoon
1 teaspoon	salt	1 teaspoon
1½–2 kg	fresh roasting chicken	3–4 lb
2	bay leaves	2
	few strands of saffron or ⅛ teaspoon, if powdered	
2	egg yolks	2
	finely chopped coriander leaves or parsley	

Measure the coconut into a jug, pour over the boiling water and stir.

In a mortar or coffee mill grind the peppercorns with the coriander seeds until finely powdered. Mix with the cayenne pepper and salt.

Rub the spice mixture into the skin of the bird and place the chicken in a casserole. Pour over the strained coconut milk and add the bay leaves and saffron.

Cover tightly and cook in a moderate oven, 180°C, 350°F, Gas Mark 4, for about 1 hour or until the chicken is tender.

Lift out the chicken and joint it on to a serving dish. Cover and keep hot. Strain the liquid and reduce it over high heat to about 300 ml (½ pint). Whisk in the egg yolks over gentle heat to thicken the sauce but do not allow to boil.

Pour the sauce over the chicken and garnish with the chopped coriander or parsley. Serve with boiled rice.

Pork Steaks with Green Peppercorns

Serves 4

Pork is invariably good value, especially in the summer. Buy slices of boneless shoulder for this recipe. Green peppercorns, introduced by the French about fifteen years ago, are now available fresh in Waitrose branches. Take them off the stems and put them in dry sherry in a screwtop jar, and they will keep in the fridge for a month. Otherwise use canned or freeze-dried green peppercorns.

4	pork shoulder steaks	4
2 tablespoons	green peppercorns	2 tablespoons
	knob of butter	
4 tablespoons	dry cider	4 tablespoons
4 tablespoons	clotted or double cream (optional)	4 tablespoons

Bat the pork steaks until of even thickness. Crush the green peppercorns and press into both sides of each piece of meat.

The meat can be stored on a plate in the refrigerator for up to 24 hours or until ready to cook.

Melt the butter in a pan and gently cook the meat for about 5 minutes on each side or until cooked. Remove the meat and keep hot.

Pour the cider into the pan and simmer for a few minutes, mixing in the meat juices. Stir in the cream, if you wish, bringing almost to the boil. Spoon over the meat and serve.

Beef and Vegetable Pie

I've been making this pie for years and I include it at the request of my husband who recommends it for long rail and car journeys or picnics.

Wholemeal shortcrust pastry:

180 g	plain white flour	6 oz
180 g	plain wholemeal flour	6 oz
¼ teaspoon	salt	¼ teaspoon
90 g	butter or margarine	3 oz
90 g	white vegetable shortening	3 oz
6 tablespoons	cold water	6 tablespoons

Filling:

500 g	lean minced beef	1 lb
1	clove garlic, crushed	1
1	small leek, chopped	1
1	stick celery, chopped	1
1	carrot, grated	1
1	green or red pepper, seeded and diced	1
	salt, pepper	
	egg yolk, to glaze	

Measure the flours and salt into a bowl. Rub in the fats and mix to a dough with the water. Rest the pastry, wrapped, in the refrigerator.

Mix the beef with the garlic, leek, celery, carrot and green or red pepper. Add salt and pepper to season.

Roll out just over half the pastry and line a 23 cm (9 in) pie dish or tin 4 cm (1½ in) deep. Spoon the filling on to the pastry and cover with the rest of the pastry rolled out to fit.

Cut a steam vent in the centre and decorate the lid with pastry leaves cut from the trimmings. Brush the pastry with beaten egg yolk mixed with a little salt.

Bake the pie on a preheated baking sheet in the centre of a

moderately hot oven, 200°C, 400°F, Gas Mark 6, for 50–60 minutes, until the pastry is crisp and the meat is cooked. Use a meat thermometer to check if in doubt.

Either serve hot straight away or cool in the pie dish and cut into wedges when cold.

Breasts of Turkey with Cranberry and Orange Stuffing

Serves 4

Now that fresh turkey is a good value meat available all year round it is worth devising interesting ways with it. This recipe works equally well with breasts of chicken or escalopes of veal.

4	escalopes of turkey breast	4
	knob of butter	
½	small onion, chopped	½
1	stick celery, chopped	1
60 g	broken walnuts	2 oz
1	thick slice wholemeal bread	1
3 rounded tablespoons	cranberry sauce (Ocean Spray)	3 rounded tablespoons
	juice and finely grated rind of 1 orange	
	salt, pepper	
	a little beurre manié (optional)	

In turn, place each escalope in a plastic bag and bat with a mallet or rolling pin until thin.

Melt half the butter and cook the onion and celery until soft. Chop the walnuts and make the bread into bread-crumbs—do them together in a blender or processor. Add to the onion and celery with the cranberry sauce, half the grated rind of the orange, salt and pepper and mix well.

Divide the stuffing between the escalopes and spread it over the surface. Roll up the meat and arrange, flap down, in an ovenproof dish. Grate the rest of the orange rind over the meat and sprinkle with salt and pepper. Dot with the rest of the butter and pour over the juice of the orange.

Cover with buttered paper or foil and bake in a moderate oven, 180°C, 350°F, Gas Mark 4, for 30–35 minutes. If the orange sauce is too thin, thicken with a little beurre manié and pour over the meat.

Sesame Sausages

Makes about 1½ kg (3 lb)

Home-made sausages are not necessarily cheaper but they are free of unwelcome additives and are full of flavour, meat and seasoning, like sausages used to be. Roll the sausages in sesame seeds for a nutty flavour, otherwise breadcrumbs or seasoned flour work well.

1 kg	belly pork	2 lb
300 g	lean pork	10 oz
1	thick slice wholemeal bread	1
1 tablespoon	salt	1 tablespoon
	pepper	
	dash of Worcester sauce	
1	slim clove garlic, crushed	1
1–2 teaspoons	quatre épices*	1–2 teaspoons
	or	
1–2 tablespoons	chopped chives or other fresh herbs	1–2 tablespoons
few tablespoons	sesame seeds, slightly roasted	few tablespoons
	butter or oil for frying	

Remove the rind and any bones from the meat and cut into pieces.

I prefer a good old-fashioned mincer fitted with a disc of 4 mm (⅛ in) sized holes (you can use a food processor but I find it chews the meat) to mince the meat into a bowl. Leave out the bread if you want one hundred per cent meat sausages. I include just one slice to clean all the meat out of the mincer at the end.

Stir in the salt, pepper, Worcester sauce, garlic and quatre épices or herbs. Mix well and fry a teaspoonful to check the seasoning. If you have time, take my butcher's advice and chill the mixture, covered, overnight.

Take a spoonful of the mixture (commercial sausages weigh about 60 g (2 oz) each) and shape into a sausage. Roll in sesame seeds.

Fry the sausages lightly in butter or oil and finish cooking under the grill. The fat left after cooking is very good dripping.

These sausages freeze well; thaw before cooking

Quatre épices:
If you wish to make your own quatre épices, a spice mixture that is invaluable in flavouring pâtés, terrines and other cooked meat dishes, here are the proportions. These vary a little according to region. Sometimes ground ginger replaces the cinnamon and one part of the black pepper can be ground allspice, also known as Jamaica pepper in old recipe books.

> 7 parts ground black pepper
> 1 part ground nutmeg
> 1 part ground cloves
> 1 part ground cinnamon

Mix all the ingredients together and store in a small screwtop jar.

GAME
AND OFFAL

The annual fuss and attention that is lavished on the Glorious Twelfth—newsreel of a brace of sad-looking grouse free falling on to the terrace of a smart London restaurant before the day is out—has ill-served the image of game. Either regarded as way beyond their pocket or solely reserved for country squires, most shoppers scarcely contemplate buying game from one year's end to the next. Yet the truth is that a great deal of game is good value and its seasonal nature helps to give our cooking welcome variety.

I discussed with my local game dealer the order of cheapness of game. He started with rabbit, a year-round meat, through hare, which is very rich and therefore goes a long way, to venison, which varies in price throughout the country, since deer farms are now helping to lower the price somewhat. Venison has virtually no fat and is a very good buy. However it pays to marinate it (the recipe is below) and then proceed as for slow-cooked beef. Coming from fur to feather, wood pigeon is of course the cheapest, followed by wild duck, at times, and then pheasant and partridge. As in France, quail and guinea fowl are now being increasingly farmed (technically ruling them out as game, but they are usually on sale with game) which lowers their price. But grouse, snipe and woodcock must head the list for cost and unless you have your own moor (or have lovely neighbours) are bound to come expensive. I have included recipes for some of the cheaper game but if you have low-cost sources yourself you may be glad of Douglas Sutherland's charming and useful *The Colonel's Cookbook* to extend your range of recipes for this often overlooked food.

Awful is how Margaret Costa refers to offal in her excellent *Four Seasons Cookery Book* to describe how many see this meat. Unless badly cooked, offal is not at all awful. It benefits from a delicate touch—gently cooked and sensitively sauced, it is delicious: Sweetbreads with Green Peppers and Spring Onions, Calves' Liver en Brochette, Oxtail with Damsons. This is fine food and not something to pull a face over. Because so many do, though, the rest of us have the advantage of finding most of this meat extraordinarily good value.

Offal is not always on display in the butcher's, but it is

167

always worth asking about it. Animals are not yet bred lacking their kidneys, heart or tongue, although butchers' shops often look as if they were. Once again it is a matter of making a friend of your butcher. If he discovers that you are interested in all his produce he is quite likely to befriend you. A good butcher often tucks the odd trotter or a few kidneys into your bag once he knows how much you appreciate them. It is wiser, if you can, to discuss with your butcher what you want to cook and how, since he may well have some helpful comments.

Here is an excellent marinade for game and other strong meats which is slightly adapted from the recipe in Elizabeth David's *French Provincial Cooking*. Halve the recipe if appropriate.

> ½ teacup of oil, preferably olive
> ¼ – ⅓ bottle red wine or cider
> 1 onion, sliced
> 1 clove garlic, crushed
> 2 teaspoons crushed coriander seeds for venison
> *or* 1 teaspoon crushed juniper berries for hare or beef
> a sprig of thyme or marjoram
> a little ground black pepper

Mix all the ingredients together in a bowl large enough to contain the meat. Steep hare for 12 hours, a joint of venison or beef for at least 24 hours, always in a cold place or the refrigerator. Dry the meat before starting to cook and if adding the marinade, strain it first.

Rabbit with Two Mustards   *Serves 4–6*

Mustard has long been an appropriate seasoning for rabbit. I use two mustards to give a good depth of flavour to the dish.

1	rabbit, jointed	1
1 tablespoon	Dijon mustard	1 tablespoon
1 tablespoon	red wine vinegar	1 tablespoon
2 tablespoons	butter	2 tablespoons
60 g	smoked bacon, diced	2 oz
1	onion, chopped	1
1	clove garlic, crushed	1
1 tablespoon	cider vinegar	1 tablespoon
2 tablespoons	seed mustard	2 tablespoons
1	egg yolk	1
	finely chopped parsley	

If the rabbit is wild, soak it in cold salt water for 2–3 hours. If tame, just wash in cold water.

Drain the meat well and arrange the joints on a plate. Mix the Dijon mustard with the vinegar and spread the mixture over the rabbit. Chill for 4–5 hours.

Melt the butter in a pan and sauté the bacon, onion and garlic until soft. Use a slotted spoon to transfer them to a hot casserole. Quickly sear the joints of rabbit in the pan and add them to the casserole. Stir the cider vinegar into 300 ml (½ pint) cold water and pour into the pan. Bring to the boil, stirring in all the pan juices, and pour over the rabbit. Cover the casserole and cook in a moderate oven, 180°C, 350°F, Gas Mark 4, for 1–1½ hours until tender.

Lift the rabbit on to a serving dish and keep hot. Strain the sauce into a pan, stir in the seed mustard and simmer for a few minutes. Add the egg yolk to the sauce, stir until thickened, and remove from the heat before it boils.

Pour the sauce over the rabbit and sprinkle with chopped parsley.

Devilled Lambs' Kidneys   *Serves 2*

Lambs' kidneys are usually under 10p each and 3 or 4 make
a quick and delicious meal. Devilled kidneys can be cooked
as below or, if you prefer, slide halved kidneys, brushed with
the devil mixture, on to a skewer and grill.

6–8	lambs' kidneys	6–8
30 g	butter	1 oz
1	slim clove garlic, crushed	1
2–3 teaspoons	mustard powder	2–3 teaspoons
2–3 teaspoons	Worcestershire sauce	2–3 teaspoons
	salt, pepper	
	finely chopped parsley	

Cut each kidney into 4 or 5 pieces discarding the cores.

Melt the butter in a pan and cook the garlic until golden.
Add the kidneys and cook, stirring, for 3–4 minutes over
moderate heat.

In a cup, mix the mustard with the Worcestershire sauce
and stir into the pan. Cook for 3–4 minutes.

Serve, sprinkled with parsley, on hot toast or with boiled
rice—white or brown.

Pigeon Pie

Serves 6–8

In her *Food in England*, Dorothy Hartley gives details of a substantial pigeon pie that incorporates a double crust. The first suet crust becomes a kind of dumpling and is then covered with shortcrust pastry. You would certainly need to be very hungry to get through it. For today's appetites I have kept to the same ingredients but omitted the first crust.

4	pigeons	4
4	cloves	4
	salt, pepper	
	bay leaf or sliver of garlic or shredded shallot	
250 g	rump steak, thinly cut	8 oz
120 g	mushrooms	4 oz
60 g	ham or bacon trimmings	2 oz

Shortcrust pastry:

180 g	plain flour	6 oz
45 g	butter	1½ oz
45 g	lard or clarified dripping	1½ oz
3 tablespoons	cold water	3 tablespoons
	egg yolk, to glaze	

Joint the pigeons, or, as I prefer, simply cut off the breast meat and the legs. Simmer the carcases in enough water to cover with the cloves and some salt and pepper.

Place the bay leaf, garlic or shallot in the bottom of a piedish. Cover with the beef, cut in neat pieces. Arrange the jointed pigeon on top and season. Place the mushrooms and ham pieces in the gaps.

Pour over enough spiced pigeon stock to cover (save the rest for soup). Cover the dish closely with foil and bake in a moderate oven, 180°C, 350°F, Gas Mark 4, for 1 hour.

Meanwhile make the shortcrust pastry in the usual way and roll out. Cover the piedish and make a good steam vent, brush the pastry with egg yolk and bake the pie in the oven turned up to 200°C, 400°F, Gas Mark 6, for a further 30 minutes or until the pastry is crisp and golden.

171

Sweetbreads with Green Peppers and Spring Onions

Serves 4

My local butcher was selling sweetbreads in March this year at 60p per lb—good value indeed. Here I have combined them with the fresh flavour of green pepper and spring onions.

500 g	lambs' sweetbreads	1 lb
45 g	butter	1½ oz
30 g	flour	1 oz
150 ml	dry white wine	¼ pint
150 ml	water	¼ pint
2–3	spring onions	2–3
1 teaspoon	tomato paste	1 teaspoon
	salt, pepper	
1	small green pepper, seeded and diced	1
4 tablespoons	single cream	4 tablespoons

Soak the sweetbreads in cold water for 2–4 hours until all the blood has been drawn from the meat.

Cover with fresh cold water in a pan and slowly bring to the boil. Simmer for 2–3 minutes then drain and refresh in cold water. Cut away any skin or gristle and cut the sweetbreads into even sized pieces.

Melt the butter in a heavy based pan and stir in the flour for 1–2 minutes. Gradually stir in the wine and water and cook until clear and thickened. Add the sweetbreads and spring onions. Cook gently for 5 minutes.

Stir in the tomato paste and season with salt and pepper. Add the green pepper and cook for 2–3 minutes until softened.

Stir in the cream and serve with buttered rice or creamed potatoes.

Brochettes of Calves' Liver

Serves 3–4

Liver is easily ruined by overcooking—it should be cooked more in the manner of fish, gently and quickly. Calves' liver is often difficult to find. My advice is to consult Susan Campbell's invaluable *Guide to Good Food Shops*, from which I discovered a splendid butcher in Clifton where calves' liver is always available.

250–350 g	calves' liver	8–12 oz
180 g	green bacon, cut in strips	6 oz
180 g	small mushrooms	6 oz
8	bay leaves	8
	olive or sunflower oil	
	salt, pepper	

Cut the liver in thin strips and then again to give even pieces. Thread the liver on to skewers, allowing one skewer for each person. Alternate the liver with pieces of bacon, which can be rolled if easier, and the mushrooms. Add a bay leaf now and again.

Place the skewers on a plate and brush with a little olive oil. Grind some salt and pepper over them.

Cook at the last moment under a moderate grill for 8–10 minutes, turning when necessary.

Serve on a bed of creamed potatoes, boiled rice or Piperade (see p. 90).

Variation: grill a brochette of pieces of calves' liver alternated with slices of fresh mango for a fine summer dish.

Onions Stuffed with Kidneys   *Serves 4*

A reviving dish, popular with sailors in Southampton inns during the last century. Although not obligatory, I like the nautical touch of rum.

4	large Spanish onions	4
4	lambs' kidneys	4
	salt, pepper	
	a tot of rum (optional)	
60 g	butter	2 oz
	fresh herbs, chopped	
300 ml	beef stock	½ pint

Peel and trim the onions. Slice a lid from the base of each onion and, using a sharp vegetable knife, remove the centre of the onion to make a hole large enough for a kidney. Skin the kidneys and remove the cores.

Season the onions with salt and black pepper and place a kidney in each. Pour over a little rum if you are a sea-dog, add a knob of butter and replace the lid.

Arrange the stuffed onions, preferably supporting each other, in a fireproof dish. Scatter with herbs and pour in the stock. If more convenient, wrap each onion in foil to cook. Bake in a moderate oven, 180°C, 350°F, Gas Mark 4, for about 1 hour, until the onions are just cooked. Serve with hot crusty bread.

Brawn

How to make the most of the less popular parts of an animal such as the head, tail or feet can be a puzzle to freezer owners who buy their meat by the half animal. It is traditional to make brawn with a pig's head and when well made, it is delicious. My mother's trick is to add plenty of parsley to the jelly, which lightens and freshens the flavour of the brawn.

½	pig's head	½
2	onions, each stuck with 6 cloves	2
2	carrots, chopped	2
1	leek, chopped (not essential)	1
1	stick of celery, chopped	1
	bunch of pot herbs	
	few peppercorns	
	salt	
1	tumbler of dry cider	1
	strip of lemon peel	
4–6 tablespoons	chopped parsley	4–6 tablespoons

Quickly rinse the head in cold water. It is easier to fit into a pan if cut into three by the butcher. Put into a pan with the cloved onions, carrots, leek and celery. Add the herbs, peppercorns, and only a little salt because the stock is reduced later. Cover with water and add the cider.

Bring to the boil and skim off any froth. Turn down the heat and simmer the pan for about 3 hours or until the meat parts easily from the bone. Remove the meat and strain the liquor into a bowl.

Pour the liquor back into the pan, add the lemon peel and reduce by half. Taste, check the seasoning and leave to cool slightly.

Meanwhile discard the vegetables and bones and cut the meat into small pieces.

Stir the parsley into the stock and pour over the meat.

Spoon into a chilled bowl and leave in a cold place to set.

Dip the bowl or mould briefly in hot water and unmould the brawn on to a serving dish. Cut into slices to serve as a first or main course.

La Gougère with Turkey Livers in Red Wine

Serves 4

Here is an appetising lunch or supper dish. A gougère is a light choux pastry which includes cheese; simple to do and excellent but bring it to the table as soon as it is cooked.

75 g	plain flour	2½ oz
	salt, pepper	
150 ml	boiling water	¼ pint
60 g	butter	2 oz
2	eggs	2
60 g	Gruyère cheese, finely diced	2 oz

Filling:

250 g	turkey livers	8 oz
1	shallot or small onion, chopped	1
	knob of butter	
20 g	flour	¾ oz
½ teaspoon	tomato paste	½ teaspoon
1	wine glass red wine, preferably a cheaper Burgundy	1
150 ml	stock or water	¼ pint
	salt, pepper	
	chopped chives or parsley	

Butter a 25 cm (10 in) white china flan dish and place a baking sheet in a moderately hot oven, 200°C, 400°F, Gas Mark 6.

Sieve the flour with a little salt and some pepper on to a sheet of greaseproof paper.

Measure the water into a heavy based pan and add the butter cut in pieces. When the butter has melted bring the water back to the boil. Remove from the heat and immediately add all the flour and then beat, over moderate heat, until the mixture leaves the sides of the pan.

Turn the mixture into a warmed bowl and add the eggs, one at a time, beating each in well. (This is far easier with an electric beater, fixed or hand-held.) Finally stir in almost all the cheese.

Place spoonfuls of the mixture around the edge of the flan dish, leaving a space in the centre. Scatter the rest of the cheese on the pastry.

Bake on the preheated baking sheet in the centre of the oven for 35 minutes.

Meanwhile prepare the filling. Cut the turkey livers into neat pieces, discarding any skin or fat. Cook the shallot in the butter until golden. Add the turkey livers and turn over in the butter until they have changed colour. Stir in the flour and tomato paste and then the wine and stock. Season and cook, stirring all the time until thickened. Simmer over very low heat until the gougère is ready.

Spoon the filling into the centre of the gougère and sprinkle with chives or parsley.

Lambs' Livers with Dill Cucumber and Cream
Serves 3–4

Prepared and cooked in a trice, this dish gets away from the all too familiar liver and bacon taste.

350 g	lambs' liver	12 oz
30 g	butter	1 oz
1	fat clove of garlic, crushed	1
6	pickled dill cucumbers, sliced	6
2 tablespoons	sultanas	2 tablespoons
	juice of 1 lemon	
6 tablespoons	double cream	6 tablespoons

Slice the liver into narrow strips. Melt the butter in a pan and cook the garlic until just golden.

Gently sauté the liver in the butter, stirring from time to time, for 3–4 minutes until cooked.

Add the dill cucumbers, sultanas and lemon juice. Simmer for 3–4 minutes. Stir in the cream and bring almost to the boil. Serve straight away with rice or noodles.

Poached Pheasant with Celery Sauce

Serves 4

If you live in the country or visit it fairly often pheasant can be had very cheaply, and even more so if you shoot. Most people seem to roast pheasant, but I think they cook better in a casserole. This appealing method of preparing pheasant is from Ruth Lowinsky's post-war austerity book, *Food for Pleasure*.

1	plump pheasant	1
about 600 ml	light stock	about 1 pint
1	carrot, chopped	1
1	onion, quartered	1
2	cloves	2
	bouquet of parsley	
	salt, few peppercorns	

Celery sauce:

4	sticks white tender celery	4
60 g	butter	2 oz
1	onion, chopped	1
	faggot of parsley stalks	
	bay leaf	
	sprig of fresh thyme	
1	clove	1
150 ml	light stock	¼ pint
30 g	flour	1 oz
	salt, pepper	
150 ml	single cream (if available)	¼ pint

Truss the pheasant and place in a stew pan or covered casserole. Pour in the stock to just cover. Add the carrot, onion, cloves, parsley, salt and peppercorns.

Simmer gently on the hob or in a moderate oven, 180°C, 350°F, Gas Mark 4, for 50–60 minutes or until tender.

Meanwhile wash the celery well. Chop and put in a pan with an egg-sized piece of the butter. Add the onion, parsley, bay leaf, thyme and clove. Cook gently, covered, for 10 minutes. Pour in the stock and cook until tender.

Extract the parsley stalks, bay leaf and clove and reduce the contents of the pan to a purée in a processor or Mouli.

Melt the rest of the butter in the pan and stir in the flour. Pour the purée back and cook, stirring all the time, until thickened. Season, add the cream and keep hot.

Remove the pheasant (keep the stock and vegetables for soup) and carve on to a hot serving dish. Pour over the celery sauce which should be quite thick.

Hearts under Lemon Walnut Stuffing

Serves 4

Hearts have always been popular in budget eating and not only in the home. Some years ago André Simon wrote that thinly sliced calves' heart was sometimes passed off as wild duck in some Soho restaurants. At the time of writing sheep's hearts can be bought for 30 pence each. Rather than stuffing them whole, I find they taste better sliced and cooked under a savoury stuffing to keep the meat moist.

3 or 4	sheep's hearts	3 or 4
1–2 tablespoons	good dripping or butter	1–2 tablespoons
1	lemon	1
1	onion, finely chopped	1
1	stick of celery, chopped	1
30 g	walnuts, chopped	1 oz
120 g	wholemeal breadcrumbs	4 oz
	salt, pepper	
3–4 tablespoons	top of milk	3–4 tablespoons

Cut each heart in half and slice thinly, discarding the outer skin and any pipes or fat. Give all this to the cat, who will love it.

Melt a little fat in a pan and gently sear the sliced heart on both sides. Remove to a hot shallow oven dish. Squeeze the juice of the lemon into the pan, swill round and pour over the meat.

Soften the onion and celery in the rest of the fat. Turn into a bowl with the walnuts, breadcrumbs, the grated rind of the lemon, salt and pepper.

Mix in the milk, making the stuffing wet enough to hold together.

Spread the stuffing over the meat. Cover with a buttered paper and bake in a moderate oven, 180°C, 350°F, Gas Mark 4, for about 1½ hours, until the meat is tender and the stuffing is crisp on top. Serve with puréed potatoes or Colcannon (see p. 116).

Harvest Pie

Look out for fresh rabbit. I am sometimes able to intercept
one of the many *en route* to France from English rabbit
farmers. *Watership Down* and memories of myxomatosis
seem to have finished off our native appetite for this excellent
meat.

1	large or 2 small rabbits, jointed	1
	salt, pepper	
8–12	slices smoked streaky bacon	8–12
300 ml	dry cider	½ pint
300 ml	cold water	½ pint

Forcemeat balls:

120 g	fresh white breadcrumbs	4 oz
60 g	suet or butter, grated	2 oz
60 g	bacon, finely chopped	2 oz
1 tablespoon	fresh herbs, mainly chives, parsley and thyme	1 tablespoon
1	large egg	1
1	small lemon	1
	butter, for frying	
350 g	puff pastry	12 oz
	egg yolk, to glaze	

Wrap a slice of bacon around each seasoned joint of rabbit.
Arrange them in a single layer in a pie dish.

Mix the cider with the water and pour over the meat. Cook,
covered, in a moderate oven, 180°C, 350°F, Gas Mark 4, for
1 hour.

Meanwhile make the forcemeat balls. Mix all the ingredients, except the butter for frying, together in a bowl. The
mixture should be moist enough to shape into small balls the
size of a walnut. Fry them in melted butter and set aside to
cool.

Remove the pie dish from the oven and add the forcemeat
balls, scattering them amongst the joints of rabbit.

Roll out the pastry to fit the pie dish, trim and crimp the edges. Decorate the pie with leaves made from the pastry trimmings and make 2 or 3 steam vents. Brush with egg yolk and replace in the oven, turned up to 200°C, 400°F, Gas Mark 6, for 30–40 minutes, until the pastry is crisp and the rabbit is tender.

Stuffed Green Peppers
with Tomato Sauce

Serves 3–4

Here is my approximation of a delicious lunch we ate years ago in a restaurant in Austria. Locally grown green peppers are often exceedingly good value from July to October.

6–8	green peppers	6–8
1 tablespoon	olive or sunflower oil	1 tablespoon
1	medium onion, chopped	1
1	clove of garlic, crushed	1
4	rashers smoked streaky bacon, chopped	4
180–250 g	chicken livers, chopped	6–8 oz
1 tablespoon	ground cumin	1 tablespoon
1 teaspoon	ground coriander	1 teaspoon
	salt, pepper	
2 teacups	boiled rice	2 teacups
6–8	bay leaves, fresh if possible	6–8
150 ml	chicken stock or water	¼ pint

Fresh tomato sauce with mint and basil:

½ kg	ripe tomatoes, skinned	1 lb
2 teaspoons	flour	2 teaspoons
2 teaspoons	sugar	2 teaspoons
	good pinch celery salt	
	salt, pepper	
1 tablespoon	chopped fresh mint	1 tablespoon
1 teaspoon	chopped fresh basil	1 teaspoon

Use a vegetable knife to cut around and remove the stem of each green pepper. Discard the seeds and any membrane and rinse out the pepper with cold water. Arrange them, so close that they support each other, upright in a lidded casserole.

Heat the oil in a pan and fry the onion and garlic with the bacon for 3 minutes. Add the chopped chicken livers and cook gently for 4–5 minutes.

Stir in the cumin, coriander, some salt and pepper and the rice. When everything is well combined, spoon the mixture into the peppers. Pack down fairly tightly and cover the top of each pepper with a bay leaf with each end tucked down into the filling.

Pour the stock around the stuffed peppers, cover tightly, and cook in a moderate oven, 180°C, 350°F, Gas Mark 4, for 40 minutes.

Meanwhile make the sauce. Sieve the skinned tomatoes into a saucepan. Blend in the flour and sugar and add the celery salt plus a little salt and pepper. Bring to the boil. Add the herbs and simmer the sauce for 8–10 minutes.

Lift the stuffed peppers on to a hot serving dish and pour the tomato sauce over them.

Nahe Valley Venison
Serves 8–10

Our friends in Rheinland-Pfalz served us this succulent venison dish as a farewell meal at the end of one of our holidays there. Venison is highly regarded in Germany while here, only Scotland seems to have the sense to share that opinion.

2–3 kg	joint of venison for roasting	4–6 lb
1	onion, finely chopped	1
1	clove garlic, crushed	1
1 tablespoon	dark brown sugar	1 tablespoon
12	black peppercorns, crushed	12
¼ teaspoon	ground cloves	¼ teaspoon
3 tablespoons	olive or sunflower oil	3 tablespoons
2 wine glasses	local red wine or port	2 wine glasses
	salt	
about 300 ml	beef or ham stock	about ½ pint
1 tablespoon	each of butter and flour blended together to make beurre manié	1 tablespoon

In a bowl large enough to contain the venison, mix the onion, garlic, sugar, peppercorns, cloves, oil and wine. Turn the meat over in the marinade to coat it. Cover closely with Clingfilm and chill for 3–4 days, turning the meat over in the marinade every day.

To roast the meat, line a roasting tin with aluminium foil, leaving enough sticking out to enclose the meat. Place the joint on the foil, sprinkle with salt and spoon the marinade over and around the meat. Wrap the foil securely over the meat, pressing the joins together.

Roast the venison in a slow oven, 160°C, 325°F, Gas Mark 3, allowing 30 minutes per ½ kg (per pound). The meat is cooked when a skewer penetrates the thickest piece easily.

Unwrap the meat enough to strain off the meat juices. Rewrap the venison and keep hot until ready to serve.

Make up the meat juices to about ½ litre (¾ pint) with the stock. Pour into a pan and simmer for a few minutes. Gradually beat in the beurre manié in small pieces and cook the sauce until thickened and glossy. You may need to add a dash of wine to revive the colour. The consistency should not be too thick. Check the seasoning and pour into a jug or bowl for serving.

Carve the venison into slices and serve with the sauce, some rowan or crab apple or other sharp jelly and hot buttered noodles.

Pressed Tongue in Wine Jelly

Serves 6 upwards

Tongue is a rich meat which will feed a good number, especially if served with cold chicken or turkey. Most butchers sell ox tongue brined and sometimes smoked. Follow his instructions on any necessary soaking.

1	ox tongue	1
2	pig's trotters	2
1	onion, stuck with cloves	1
1	carrot, chopped	1
1	stick of celery, chopped	1
	bouquet of fresh herbs	
8	peppercorns	8
150 ml	red wine	¼ pint

Place the tongue in a pan and cover with cold water. Add the trotters, onion, carrot, celery, herbs and peppercorns and bring to the boil. Cover and lower the heat so that the water just shivers. Cook gently on the hob or in the oven for 3–4 hours until a skewer will pierce the meat easily.

Lift out the tongue and skin it while hot, removing any little bones or gristle at the same time.

Strain the stock and return to the pan with the wine. Reduce over high heat until it measures 900 ml (1½ pints). Taste to check the flavour and correct the seasoning.

Cut the tongue in half lengthways and place one piece, cut side down, in a straight-sided cake tin or a soufflé dish, curling it round neatly. Place the other half on top, cut side up.

Pour over the slightly cooled stock and place a weighted plate on top of the meat to press it into shape. Leave overnight in a cold place to set.

Remove the weighted plate and wrap a hot damp cloth around the mould. Invert on to a flat serving plate and slice thinly across.

Rabbit with White Cabbage and Juniper Berries

Serves 4

If you mention cabbage to most people a pained look records their reaction. Perhaps it is a common memory of soggy school cabbage that insulates us from interesting experiments with this much-maligned vegetable. Determined to rid myself of this attitude, I set out deliberately each season to devise good ways with cabbage—this is one I recommend.

1 kg	rabbit, jointed	2–3 lb
	seasoned flour	
2–3 tablespoons	dripping	2–3 tablespoons
1	onion, sliced	1
1	clove garlic, finely chopped	1
1 teaspoon or 24	juniper berries, bruised	1 teaspoon or 24
150 ml	½ cider/½ stock or water	¼ pint
500 g	white cabbage	1 lb
	salt, pepper	

Soak wild rabbit in salt water for 2–3 hours; if tame simply wipe with a damp cloth.

Dry the rabbit and roll in seasoned flour. Heat the dripping and brown each piece of rabbit. Remove the joints and keep hot.

Cook the onion and garlic in the pan for a few minutes. Add the juniper berries and the cider and stock mixture. Simmer for 3 minutes.

Meanwhile, slice the cabbage finely. Blanch in boiling salted water for 3–4 minutes. Drain well and turn into the base of a hot casserole. Season with salt and pepper.

Place the rabbit on top and pour in the juniper flavoured stock.

Cover tightly and cook in a slow oven, 160°C, 325°F, Gas Mark 3, for about 1½ hours or until the rabbit is tender and the cabbage has absorbed the cooking juices.

Jugged Hare

As I write, a splendid brown hare that I have just bought in Tiverton market hangs head down in my cool room. To cook it in this most traditional way, you can use a jug (stoneware is best) but an earthenware or cast iron casserole works just as well. Not only is hare good value but with its strong flavour a small amount satisfies. Because jugged hare reheats so well, it is a good dish for a party, and it can be extended by adding strips of ham or gammon. Don't be put off by what look like endless ingredients—everything is very straightforward.

Marinade:

150 ml	red wine	¼ pint
2 tablespoons	sunflower oil	2 tablespoons
1	onion, thinly sliced	1
2	bay leaves	2
	small bunch fresh thyme or a little dried	
6	juniper berries, crushed	6
6	black peppercorns, crushed	6
¼ teaspoon	salt	¼ teaspoon
1	hare, with blood if possible	1
1 tablespoon	bacon fat	1 tablespoon
2	onions, each stuck with 3 cloves	2
1	stick celery, chopped	1
1	carrot, chopped	1
	bouquet garni, fresh or dried	
	strip of lemon rind	
8	allspice berries, crushed	8
6	black peppercorns, crushed	6
	a little salt	
just under 1 litre	stock or water	1½ pints
1 tablespoon	redcurrant or crab apple jelly	1 tablespoon
1 tablespoon	butter and flour blended together to make beurre manié	1 tablespoon
	forcemeat balls (see recipe for Harvest Pie, p. 182)	
	watercress, for garnish	

Joint the hare and keep the blood separately in the refrigerator. Measure the ingredients for the marinade into a saucepan. Bring to the boil, remove from the heat and cool. Pour over the meat, cover and keep in the fridge for 24 hours. Turn the meat over now and again.

Drain the hare and dry it on kitchen paper. Strain the marinade into a saucepan and reduce it over high heat to half. Reserve.

Quickly sear the meat in the bacon fat and arrange the pieces in a casserole. Add the onions, celery, carrot, herbs, lemon rind, spices, seasoning and stock to the pan. Bring to the boil and pour over the hare. Cover tightly and cook in a slow oven, 150°C, 300°F, Gas Mark 2, for 2–3 hours until the meat is tender.

Strain the gravy into a saucepan, add the redcurrant jelly and the reduced marinade and bring to the boil. Add the beurre manié in small pieces and cook until thickened.

Add 2 tablespoons of the hot sauce to the blood then return it all to the sauce. Stir gently over low heat until thickened. Strain the sauce over the joints of hare arranged on a serving dish, add the hot forcemeat balls and garnish with watercress.

Oxtail with Damsons

Serves 4–6

Oxtails cooked with grapes or prunes are excellent. I find damsons go particularly well. Cook the oxtail a day ahead so that excess fat can be removed.

2	oxtails, jointed	2
	salt, pepper	
2	onions, chopped	2
1	clove garlic, chopped	1
2	carrots, chopped	2
2	sticks of celery, chopped	2
1 litre	stock or water	1¾ pints
500 g	damsons, fresh, frozen or bottled	1 lb
½	stick cinnamon	½
	bouquet of parsley stalks	

In a hot pan sear the pieces of oxtail until the fat begins to run. Remove to a hot casserole, arranging the pieces in a single layer. Season with salt and pepper.

Soften the onions and garlic in the pan in the remaining fat. Add the carrots and celery and stir around for 2–3 minutes to soften a little.

Pour in the stock and a quarter of the damsons and bring to the boil, stirring well to loosen all the pan juices. Add to the casserole and tuck in the cinnamon stick and parsley stalks. Cover tightly and cook in a slow oven, 160°C, 325°F, Gas Mark 3, for about 3 hours (this is an ideal recipe for a slo-cooker). After 2 hours check that the level of the liquid has not fallen below the meat.

When the meat parts easily from the bone, remove the casserole from the oven and pour the liquor into a jug. Chill the cooled casserole and the liquor.

Next day remove the layer of fat from the jellied liquor, turn the jelly into a pan with the rest of the damsons and simmer over moderate heat until the fruit is cooked.

Remove the cinnamon stick and parsley stalks from the casserole and reheat in the oven or over simmering water. Pour the sauce and the damsons on to the oxtail and serve. In winter creamed potatoes and in summer noodles are appropriate accompaniments.

SALADS

A good salad is a hymn to freshness and flavour; the best taste vibrant and full of goodness, made with the youngest, most tender vegetables and fruit. But I don't mean lettuce and tomato, English style, with a slice of cucumber on top. For most of the year it is hardly worth buying lettuce, tomato or cucumber. They are either ridiculously expensive or flavourless or both. Furthermore, lettuce and tomato are not usually harmonious together in a salad—they taste better as separate salads in season.

Many vegetables make fine salads once they are blanched—cauliflower, French or runner beans, or courgettes, for example. Blanch, then refresh the vegetables quickly, drain well and pour over the dressing. Others, like carrots, mangetout (far easier to grow than peas, I find) and asparagus (if possible, the best vegetable of all to grow yourself—not at all difficult and the difference in cost and improved flavour are dramatic) benefit from a brief cooking, leaving them with a hint of crispness which offsets the dressing poured over while the vegetables are still warm.

Interest in oriental and vegetarian eating has meant that an ever-growing range of pulses is appearing in health food stores. These provide unusual earthy-tasting winter salads if given a liberal dousing of well-flavoured dressing.

In the same way that most humans are much more attractive when clothed, so it is with salads. An undressed salad is not a pretty sight. So what to put on your salad? Is it wise to economise by using a blended salad oil? I think not. Although cheaper, you will rob your salads of their full potential flavour. A good oil enhances salad in manifold ways; its scent, taste, consistency and colour are all heightened.

I always buy three oils for salads: olive, walnut and sunflower. A first pressing olive oil or a little walnut oil are often all a salad needs. The flavour of both oils is so intense that very little extra seasoning is appropriate. And it is a pity to cut the rich fatness of these beautiful oils with too much lemon juice or vinegar. If your salad includes acid fruit or vegetables probably it will need oil alone, plus a grinding of salt and pepper.

For times when a well-balanced Sauce Vinaigrette is

195

required, on rice, lentils or other mild tasting ingredients, use either a combination of olive and sunflower oils or, for a salad dressing which includes plenty of garlic, sunflower oil alone may be preferable. I replace half the olive oil in Aioli with sunflower oil unless I'm making it in France, Italy or Spain where olive oil is cheaper.

Even in periods of financial stringency I am usually able to continue cooking with olive oil and butter by cutting down their use to the essential minimum and by cutting out entirely expensive methods of cooking such as deep frying which, on the whole, rarely contribute to a high standard of cuisine.

Many cooks (and cookery writers) reckon olive oil to be prohibitively expensive now. You can, however, still find good oils at a reasonable price. It certainly pays to buy as large a quantity as you can afford. Often it is worth sharing a can of oil with a friend or two. Sainsburys' olive oil, which is mild but pleasant, is cheaper than wine, and sunflower oil nearly everywhere costs less per litre than a good cider. And the oils last far longer than the drinks. I think we often talk ourselves into thinking this or that food is expensive without reading the fine print or watching how long things last in the kitchen. It is no bad idea to scribble the date of opening on various ingredients to see how economical some of them are. Or work out the cost per 30 grams or ounce of certain foods. One tends to be more aware of the hole in one's purse when buying these staples occasionally and remembering how cheap things seemed to be in the past.

I give a Sauce Vinaigrette recipe opposite. This is the classic salad dressing. However, for a fresher taste replace the wine vinegar with lemon juice, and for a thicker dressing stir in a tablespoon of thick cream.

Salad of Two Pears

Serves 4–6

Alternating spokes of avocado pear and dessert pear, doused in a Vinaigrette dressing, make an appetising first course to a winter meal. Buy the pears when still hard and bring them into a warm room to ripen when you wish.

1–2	avocado pears	1–2
1–2	dessert pears, preferably Comice	1–2
	juice of a lemon	

Sauce Vinaigrette:

1 dessertspoon	white wine vinegar salt, pepper	1 dessertspoon
3–4 tablespoons	fruity olive oil	3–4 tablespoons
2–3	spring onion tops	2–3

Quarter the avocados and gently peel off the skin. Slice the flesh lengthways on to a plate. Brush with lemon juice.

Peel and core the dessert pears. Slice thinly and brush with lemon juice.

Arrange the pear slices alternately on pretty plates like a spoked wheel.

Combine all the ingredients for the dressing in a lidded jar or small jug and shake or whisk. Pour a little over each salad.

Salad of New Potatoes
with Cucumber Dressing
Serves 4

In mid-summer cucumbers can be found for as little as 10p each. They are excellent for cooking, for soups or for this cool dressing.

500 g	new potatoes	1 lb
1	small cucumber	1
1 tablespoon	chopped fresh mint or tarragon	1 tablespoon
½ teaspoon	Dijon mustard	½ teaspoon
3–4 tablespoons	double cream	3–4 tablespoons
	juice of ½ lemon	
	pepper, salt	

Scrub or scrape the potatoes and cook in salted water until just tender.

Remove only half the peel from the cucumber with a potato peeler, finely grate the whole cucumber into a bowl. Stir in the mint or tarragon, mustard, cream and lemon juice. Season to taste with pepper and salt.

When the potatoes are cooked, remove the skins and slice into a serving dish.

Spoon over the cucumber dressing and toss slightly. Serve the salad cold, possibly with a cold fish dish or fresh sardines.

Melon Salad with Raspberry Nectarine Coulis *Serves 6–8*

The year that we built our fruit cage we were rewarded with bumper crops of raspberries, so I devised many new methods of serving them. This way tastes especially good and is very pretty.

1	large ripe melon, Honeydew, Canteloupe, Ogen, etc.	1
180 g	raspberries, fresh or frozen	6 oz
3	ripe nectarines	3
3–4 teaspoons	caster sugar	3–4 teaspoons
3 tablespoons	fruity olive oil	3 tablespoons
	a speck of salt	
	black pepper	

Cut the melon in half and remove the seeds. Take out the flesh with a melon baller or dice it with a knife. Divide the melon between individual dishes. (If you prefer, divide the melon into sections but cut the flesh into pieces for easier eating).

Purée the raspberries with the stoned nectarines (leave the skin on) and push through a fine sieve. Sweeten to taste and stir in the oil and salt with a little pepper.

Spoon the coulis over the melon and grind more black pepper on top. Serve straight away.

Rice Salad Niçoise

Serves 4–8

A good first course or main dish in a light meal.

250 g	risotto or round-grain rice	8 oz
300 ml	cold water	½ pint
½	onion, chopped	½
1	bay leaf	1
1 tablespoon	olive oil	1 tablespoon
	salt, pepper	
24	black olives	24
120 g	French beans, cooked	4 oz
2	large ripe tomatoes	2
2	eggs, hard-boiled	2
1	green pepper, seeded and diced	1
50 g	tin of anchovy fillets	1¾ oz

Dressing:

1	clove garlic, crushed	1
3–4 tablespoons	fruity olive oil	3–4 tablespoons
1 teaspoon	capers	1 teaspoon
	juice of ½ lemon	
	salt, pepper	

Tip the rice into a nylon sieve and wash under fast running cold water for 2–3 minutes. Turn the rice into a heavy based pan with the water, onion, bay leaf, olive oil, and some salt and pepper. Bring to the boil and stir. Turn down the heat to the lowest setting and cook, tightly covered, for 17 minutes.

In a good sized mixing bowl make the dressing by mixing the garlic, olive oil, capers, lemon juice, salt and pepper. Cool the rice slightly and turn into the bowl. Mix to coat the rice with the dressing. When completely cool, add the olives and beans.

Arrange the rice on a serving dish and add the quartered tomatoes and eggs around the edge. Scatter the green pepper over the salad and arrange the anchovy fillets, criss-cross fashion, on top.

Sprouted Salad

Serves 2–4

When the days are short and salad crops are expensive I resort to jam jar, muslin and elastic band to grow sprouting seeds on the kitchen windowsill. I recommend alfalfa or try mung, Aduki beans or brown rice.

Sprouted alfalfa tastes like new peas and is more unusual than mustard and cress.

> packet of sprouting seed
> 1 kilo or 2 lb wide-necked jam jar
> piece of muslin or terylene net to cover top
> elastic band
> salad dressing

Measure one tablespoon of seed into the jar. Spread the circle of cloth over the top of the jar and secure firmly with the elastic band.

Half fill the jar through the muslin with luke-warm water. Shake vigorously and then pour away the water through the cloth. Repeat twice, then leave the jar on its side, on a plate to catch drips, in a warm place until the next day.

Give the seeds a water bath, in the same way, twice a day for three days. By then the jar should be full of sprouted seed.

Simply remove the cloth and shake the contents, which will have ten times the volume of the original seed, into a salad bowl.

Pour over some salad dressing and serve.

Cauliflower Salad with Capers
and Fresh Coriander

Serves 4

Although cauliflower can, of course, be eaten raw I prefer the gentler taste of the steamed vegetable, although still with a hint of bite. This dressing is also fine for new potatoes or Jerusalem artichokes. If you can find or grow some fresh coriander (I think it benefits from glass protection) its incomparable flavour is a great addition.

1	good-sized cauliflower	1
2	hard-boiled eggs	2
½ teaspoon	Dijon mustard	½ teaspoon
generous 150 ml	olive or sunflower oil	generous ¼ pint
	finely grated rind and juice of 1 orange	
1–2 tablespoons	capers, rinsed	1–2 tablespoons
	salt, pepper	
	fresh coriander leaves or parsley	

Cut the main florets from the cauliflower and steam them, sprinkled with salt, until *just* tender. Cool a little, then arrange the florets, stalks down, in a dark-coloured serving dish.

Halve the eggs and scoop out the yolks into a bowl. Blend in the mustard and gradually add the oil as for mayonnaise. Sharpen to taste with the juice and rind of the orange and stir in the rinsed capers. Season with salt and pepper.

Spoon the dressing over the cauliflower and scatter the chopped egg whites on top. Snip the coriander or parsley leaves over the salad and serve.

Variation: to make the salad more substantial criss-cross some rinsed anchovy fillets on top and serve with brown bread.

Green Lentil Salad

Unlike red lentils which conveniently cook to a mush for soups or dhal, green and brown lentils remain separate and welcome the libation of a good dressing.

250 g	green lentils	8 oz
1	clove garlic	1
4–6 tablespoons	sunflower oil	4–6 tablespoons
1 tablespoon	wine vinegar or lemon juice	1 tablespoon
	salt, pepper	
1	onion, preferably red-skinned	1
50 g	tin of anchovy fillets *and/or*	1¾ oz
2–3	hard-boiled eggs, quartered	2–3
	handful of black olives	

Rinse the lentils in cold water, then simmer in enough water to cover until tender. This takes from 30–50 minutes depending on their age.

Drain in a sieve and refresh under cold water.

Crush the garlic into a bowl. Add the oil, vinegar, salt and pepper. Stir in the lentils and cover with the sliced onion, separated into rings.

Arrange the drained anchovies and/or eggs on top and scatter with the black olives.

This is a very filling dish: serve small portions as a first course or build the meal around it.

Avocados with Red Ginger

Serves 4

This recipe is a result of a trip to a Chinese cash and carry in Bristol where I discovered numerous exotic goodies, including a jar of red ginger. If you have a Chinese or Indian grocer near it is a good purchase for your spice cupboard, otherwise use brown preserved ginger. Serve as a first course or a salad course.

2	ripe avocado pears	2
1	clove of garlic	1
	juice of 1 orange	
1 teaspoon	clear honey	1 teaspoon
¼ teaspoon	Dijon mustard	¼ teaspoon
1 tablespoon	red preserved ginger, cut in slivers or diced	1 tablespoon
2 teaspoons	ginger syrup	2 teaspoons
	salt, pepper	

Halve the avocado pears and remove the stones. Arrange the halves in individual dishes. Alternatively peel and dice the flesh into a bowl.

Peel the garlic and spike it on a fork. In a small bowl mix the orange juice, honey and mustard with the fork. Add the preserved ginger, syrup and a little salt and pepper to taste.

Spoon over the avocados and serve.

Skordalia with Matchstick Vegetables

Serves 4 or more

A pleasing Greek alternative to mayonnaise or Aioli for serving with matchstick vegetables or crudités. By including some quartered hard-boiled eggs or cold poached fish you can construct a complete meal around this sauce.

60 g	white crustless bread	2 oz
60 g	blanched almonds	2 oz
2–3	cloves garlic, peeled	2–3
up to 150 ml	olive oil	up to ¼ pint
	squeeze of lemon juice	
	salt, pepper	

a selection of thinly cut fresh vegetables: carrots, green and red peppers, tomatoes, cucumbers, radishes, young courgettes, etc.

Soak the bread in cold water for a few minutes. Meanwhile chop the almonds in a processor or blender. Add the bread squeezed free of water and the crushed garlic. Blend together until well mixed.

Gradually add the oil through the lid, very slowly at first, and mix until of the right consistency. Sharpen with lemon juice and season with salt and pepper to taste.

Serve in a bowl surrounded by a selection of vegetables.

Jellied Summer Bortsch

Serves 6

Amongst the green and leafy salads of summer a jellied ruby-red bortsch is immediately attractive. Ideal for a party since it is best prepared well ahead.

500 g	raw beetroot, peeled and chopped	1 lb
1	carrot, sliced	1
1	stick celery, chopped	1
	white part of 1 leek	
1	small onion, chopped	1
about 1 litre	water	1¾ pints
	bunch of thyme	
	salt	
300 ml	good jellied beef stock or consommé	½ pint
1½ tablespoons	powdered gelatine	1½ tablespoons
	the juice of 1 lemon	
	splash of red wine	
	soured cream for serving (optional)	

Cook the beetroot with the carrot, celery, leek and onion in the water with the thyme and some salt for 30–40 minutes or until the beetroot is cooked.

Add the beef stock and simmer for 5 minutes. Soften the gelatine in the lemon juice and red wine in a large jug and strain the liquid from the pan on to it. Reserve the vegetables. Stir until dissolved. There should be about 1 litre (1¾ pints). Cool the liquid by standing the jug in cold water, then chill until just starting to set.

Select some of the reserved vegetables and arrange in a dish or small moulds. Pour over a little jellied bortsch and chill until firm. Continue filling the dish or moulds in this way—it is a matter of choice how much vegetable you include. I sometimes enrich the bortsch with sliced hard-boiled eggs or slivers of ham, some baby gherkins and chopped spring onions, as a change.

Chill the bortsch until set. Serve, spooned from the bowl or turn out the moulds with a garnish of lambs' lettuce or watercress. Spoon over some sour cream if you wish.

Seafood Pasta Salad

Serves 4–6

Smoked fish and pasta make good companions. This salad
makes an appetising start to a summer meal.

120 g	pasta shells, twistetti, or whatever you wish	4 oz
	splash of sunflower oil	
	sliver of garlic, crushed	
½ teaspoon	Dijon mustard	½ teaspoon
3–4 tablespoons	olive oil	3–4 tablespoons
	finely grated rind and juice of 1 lemon	
	salt, pepper	
	handful of mangetout, cooked	
2 or 3	spring onions or shallot tops, chopped	2 or 3
1	red pepper, skinned and diced	1
180 g	smoked eel or trout, skinned and cut into pieces	6 oz
1	smoked whiting, cooked and flaked	1
	handful of flat parsley, chopped	

Cook the pasta in boiling salted water with a splash of oil until
just tender. Turn into a colander, rinse under cold water and
then drain well.

In a mixing bowl, mix the crushed garlic, mustard, oil,
lemon rind and juice. Season with salt and pepper.

Turn the pasta into the bowl and toss to coat with the
dressing. Add the mangetout, spring onions, red pepper,
smoked eel or trout and whiting and toss gently. Turn on to a
serving dish and scatter with chopped parsley.

Seven Bean Salad
with Garlic Lemon Dressing   *Serves 4*

Protein rich, but cheap, dried beans have bootstrapped themselves into nearly everyone's diet. They do, however, need
a boldly flavoured dressing or sauce because, in truth, they
taste of little themselves. Most health food or vegetarian
shops sell all the beans below.

1 tablespoon of each of the following:

haricot beans	soya beans
red kidney beans	aduki beans
black eyed beans	mung beans
pink coco beans	

1 clove garlic
1 bay leaf

Dressing:

1	large clove garlic, crushed	1
	salt, pepper	
5–6 tablespoons	sunflower oil	5–6 tablespoons
	juice of 1 small lemon	
2–3 handfuls	mixed fresh herbs, finely chopped—parsley, mint, chives, chervil, etc.	2–3 handfuls

For 4 people take a tablespoon of each kind of bean. Soak all
the beans for a few hours in cold water.

Pour off the water and cover with fresh water in a pan. Add
the clove of garlic and the bay leaf, bring to the boil and
simmer fast for 10 minutes.

Lower the heat and cook, covered, until tender but not
mushy. Alternatively, pour off the cooking water after 10
minutes' fast cooking and steam the beans until cooked.
Beans take from 30–45 minutes to cook usually but it depends
on the age of the beans.

Drain the beans and rinse in cold water, then drain again.

In a large bowl, crush the garlic with the salt. Add some

milled pepper, oil and lemon juice and mix well. Stir in the chopped herbs.

Add the beans and toss in the dressing until well coated. Leave for at least 45 minutes for the beans to absorb the flavour of the dressing.

Winter Cabbage Salad

Serves 6

Most effective with three kinds of cabbage, this salad is also very good with just one. The dressing works well on shredded iceberg lettuce in the summer.

¼	medium size red cabbage	¼
¼	medium size white cabbage	¼
1	small head tender green cabbage —January King or Primo	1

Dressing:

150 ml	natural unflavoured yoghurt	¼ pint
1	sliver of garlic, crushed (optional)	1
1 tablespoon	olive oil	1 tablespoon
1½ teaspoons	Dijon mustard	1½ teaspoons
1 teaspoon	clear honey	1 teaspoon
	salt, pepper	
2 tablespoons	roasted salted peanuts, finely chopped	2 tablespoons
	a little cayenne pepper	

Shred each cabbage and soak in ice-cold water in separate bowls for 30 minutes. Drain well and turn all the cabbage into a good sized salad bowl.

Mix the yoghurt, garlic, oil, Dijon mustard and honey together in a jug or bowl. Season to taste with salt and pepper. Pour the dressing over the cabbage and toss gently to coat it.

Sprinkle the chopped nuts on top and dust with a little cayenne pepper.

Tabouleh

Serves 6–8

A Middle Eastern dish with a base of bulgar wheat or burghul, which has an earthy wholemeal taste, akin to brown rice. It is available in health food shops.

1 tablespoon	olive or sunflower oil	1 tablespoon
1 teacup*	bulgar wheat	1 teacup
2 teacups	cold water	2 teacups
3–4 tablespoons	fruity olive oil	3–4 tablespoons
	juice of 1 large lemon	
	salt, pepper	
1 bunch	spring onions, finely chopped	1 bunch
½ teacup	finely chopped parsley	½ teacup
1 tablespoon	finely chopped mint	1 tablespoon
1	crisp lettuce	1
	black olives (optional)	
	a sliced lemon (optional)	

Heat the oil in a heavy based pan. Stir in the dry bulgar wheat and then the water. Bring to the boil, stir, and lower the heat. Cover tightly and cook for 18 minutes.

In a large bowl combine the oil, lemon juice and salt and pepper. Slightly cool the cooked bulgar wheat and then mix into the bowl, making sure that all the grains are coated with the dressing.

When cool mix in the chopped onions, parsley and mint.

Serve in dishes lined with lettuce leaves. If you wish, stud the tabouleh with black olives and thinly sliced lemon.

*I use a 150 ml (¼ pint) teacup but this recipe is fairly flexible.

Green Salad with Avocado Dressing

Serves 4

A good way of serving just one avocado pear to four people.

1	small crisp lettuce	1
	few leaves of spinach, sorrel, sweet rocket and lambs' lettuce	
½	cucumber	½
1	ripe avocado pear	1
3–4 tablespoons	mayonnaise, soured cream or fromage frais	3–4 tablespoons
	salt, pepper	
	squeeze of lemon juice	
2 tablespoons	finely chopped mixed fresh herbs	2 tablespoons

Cover all the green stuff with iced water for 30 minutes. Drain well and pat dry on a cloth.

Arrange the lettuce on a chilled platter and cut the spinach, sorrel and sweet rocket into ribbons. Scatter them over the lettuce with the leaves of lambs' lettuce.

Peel the cucumber and remove the seeds. Cut the flesh into long narrow wedges.

Mash the peeled avocado until smooth and beat in the mayonnaise, soured cream or fromage frais. Season and sharpen with lemon juice.

Spoon the dressing into the centre of the salad. Arrange the cucumber wedges around the dressing and scatter the finely chopped herbs over the top.

Parsnip and Parsley Mousse   *Serves 4–6*

A delicately flavoured, cool, first course or salad course for winter meals.

350 g	parsnip, peeled and chopped	12 oz
150 ml	half milk/half water	¼ pint
	salt	
1 tablespoon	powdered gelatine	1 tablespoon
4 tablespoons	cold water or the juice of 1 lemon	4 tablespoons
2 tablespoons	finely chopped parsley	2 tablespoons
150 ml	whipping cream	¼ pint
2	egg whites	2
1	small tomato or ¼ cucumber or some watercress	1
	few sprigs of parsley	

Cook the parsnip in the milk and water with a little salt in a covered pan until tender. Purée the contents of the pan in a blender or processor.

Soften the gelatine in the water or lemon juice and then dissolve over low heat. Add to the purée, stirring, in a thin trickle and mix in the parsley.

Whip the cream and in a separate bowl whisk the egg whites until stiff. Fold the purée into the cream and then incorporate the egg whites.

Pour the mixture into 4 or 6 wetted bowls or cups and chill until set. Dip each mould briefly in hot water and unmould on to a small plate. Decorate each mousse with halved slices of tomato or cucumber or a few leaves of watercress and press a sprig of parsley on top.

Serve at room temperature or only just chilled.

Tomatoes Stuffed with Fennel and Walnuts

Serves 4

In a good tomato year, come mid-season when the sun has developed their flavour, tomatoes are often very cheap and large enough to be worth stuffing. But it is important to skin them first.

8	ripe tomatoes	8
	salt, pepper	
120 g	cream cheese	4 oz
	a little top of milk	
1 teaspoon	ground coriander	1 teaspoon
1–2 tablespoons	chopped parsley	1–2 tablespoons
1	head Florentine fennel	1
1 tablespoon	broken walnuts, chopped	1 tablespoon
	a little Sauce Vinaigrette	
	or walnut oil	
	chopped chives	

Cover the tomatoes with boiling water for ½ minute. Pour away the hot water and replace with cold water. Nick the skin of each tomato with a sharp knife. If the tomatoes are ripe it should be easy to peel away the skins.

Cut a slice from the base of each tomato to use as a lid. Scrape out the seeds and core of each tomato and rest them upside down on a wire rack to drain. Then sprinkle a little salt and pepper inside them.

Mix the cream cheese, top of milk, coriander and parsley together and season to taste with salt and pepper. Combine with the chopped fennel and walnuts.

Spoon the mixture into the tomatoes and replace the lids. Arrange the tomatoes on a serving dish and pour a little Sauce Vinaigrette or oil over them. Chill for an hour. Sprinkle the tops with chives and serve with hot French bread.

Russian Salad

Serves 7–8

Worlds apart from the substance sold under the same name in tins and cartons. This delicious salad comes from *The Russian Cookbook* by Nina Nicolaieff and Nancy Phelan.

2 cups	cooked diced potatoes	2 cups
1 cup	cooked diced beetroot	1 cup
1 cup	cooked diced carrot	1 cup
½ cup	cucumber, sliced, salted and drained	½ cup
¼ cup	finely chopped onion	¼ cup
½ cup	fresh diced cooking apple	½ cup
	salt, pepper	
	soured cream *or* mayonnaise *or* Sauce Vinaigrette	
2	hard-boiled eggs	2
about 10	lettuce leaves	about 10

In a large bowl put the potatoes, beetroot, carrot, cucumber, onion and apple. Season and then pour over your chosen dressing. Mix together carefully, trying not to break up the diced vegetables.

Turn into a glass dish or plate and arrange the lettuce leaves round. Make a daisy pattern on top, using the yolk of egg as a centre and cutting the whites to make 6 or 8 petals. Serve cold.

Variation: to make a more substantial dish add pieces of cold meat, poultry or fish or finely chopped herring.

Jerusalem Artichoke Mousse
with Hazelnut Dressing   *Serves 6–8*

This creamy-white mousse is a delight with its hauntingly delicate flavour.

¾ kg	Jerusalem artichokes, peeled	1½ lb
150 ml	water	¼ pint
300 ml	milk	½ pint
	salt	
½	small onion, sliced	½
	sliver of garlic	
	bay leaf	
20 g	flour	¾ oz
	pepper	
4 teaspoons	powdered gelatine	4 teaspoons
	juice of 1 lemon	
2 tablespoons	mayonnaise	2 tablespoons
2	egg whites	2
150 ml	whipping cream, whipped	¼ pint
	few slices unpeeled cucumber	
60 g	hazelnuts	2 oz
2–3 tablespoons	mild olive oil or sunflower oil	2–3 tablespoons
1 tablespoon	chopped parsley	1 tablespoon

Cut the artichokes into walnut-sized pieces and cook in the water with half the milk and some salt. This takes 7–10 minutes, depending on how long the artichokes have been out of the ground.

Meanwhile heat the rest of the milk in a double boiler with the onion, garlic and bay leaf.

When the artichokes are tender, pour their liquor into the seasoned milk and remove the onion, garlic and bay leaf. Purée or sieve the artichokes with a little of the milk if necessary.

Blend the flour with a little cold milk and add to the hot milk. Cook, stirring, until thickened. Check the seasoning and add some milled pepper. Strain into the purée and cool.

Soften the gelatine in the juice of half the lemon, then heat until dissolved. Add to the purée in a long thin stream, then add the mayonnaise.

Whisk the egg whites until stiff, and fold into the artichoke mixture alternately with the whipped cream.

Pour into a lightly oiled 1 litre (1¾ pint) ring mould. Chill until set. When ready to serve, dip the mould briefly in hot water and unmould the ring on to a flat plate. Cut the cucumber slices in half and arrange them cut side down around the base of the mousse.

Toast the hazelnuts and rub off the brown skin with a cloth. Roughly chop or flake the nuts. Cook the nuts in the oil for 3–4 minutes until lightly coloured. Pour into a bowl and mix in the rest of the lemon juice and the parsley. Spoon over the mousse and serve.

Broad Bean Purée with Savory   *Serves 4–6*

A good recipe for slightly older broad beans at the end of the season. Serve this hot with meat or fish or cold as part of a salad or hors d'oeuvres.

500 g	broad beans, shelled	1 lb
1–2 tablespoons	summer savory preferably, otherwise winter	1–2 tablespoons
	lemon juice	
	salt, pepper	
2–4 tablespoons	soured cream or mayonnaise	2–4 tablespoons
1 tablespoon	chopped parsley	1 tablespoon

Cook or steam the beans in salted water with half the savory. If the eye of the bean (where it is attached to the pod) is not green, cook the beans until the skins are easily detached. Remove the skins and discard.

Turn the beans into a processor with the rest of the savory and some lemon juice. Season with pepper and whizz to a purée.

If serving hot, stir in the soured cream and sprinkle with chopped parsley.

For serving cold, allow the purée to cool slightly, then mix in the mayonnaise. Turn into a dish, smooth the top and mark radially with the blade of a knife.

Caesar Salad

Serves 4–6

A great American classic. Assembling this salad can be a spectator sport, performed at the table. If possible, use a huge shallow wooden bowl. For a delightful account of Caesar Cardini, the originator, see *From Julia Child's Kitchen*.

1	cos or iceberg lettuce	1
100 ml	olive or sunflower oil	3–4 fl oz
1	slim clove garlic, crushed	1
	salt, pepper	
	juice of ½ lemon	
1	egg, boiled for 1 minute only	1
	dash of Worcester sauce	
	or	
3–4	anchovy fillets, chopped	3–4
30 g	Parmesan cheese, finely grated	1 oz
2 slices	wholemeal bread, made into croûtons	2 slices

Wash and dry the lettuce well. If the salad is not for eating straight away, chill the lettuce in a covered plastic box in the crisper of the refrigerator. Mix the oil with the garlic and whisk or shake so that the flavours combine.

Have a salad bowl ready and assemble all the other ingredients. Tear the lettuce in the bowl. Mix some salt and pepper into the oil and pour over the lettuce. Toss gently to ensure it is coated with oil.

Squeeze the juice of the lemon over the lettuce and break the egg over and toss again. Now add the Worcester sauce or the anchovy fillets (which I prefer) and cheese and toss. Finally add the cooled croûtons and toss. Serve straight away.

Iceberg Lettuce with Fruit

Serves 4–6

By including fruit there is usually no need for further acid in the dressing for this salad; just trickle the oil over everything.

1	iceberg lettuce	1
120 g	black grapes	4 oz
1	eating apple	1
1	dessert pear	1
1	sweet orange	1
	salt, pepper	
3–4 tablespoons	olive or walnut oil	3–4 tablespoons

Wash the lettuce and dry on a cloth. Arrange the leaves on a serving dish.

Halve the grapes and remove the pips. Slice the cored apple and dice the pear. Peel the orange and cut the segments free of skin.

Place the fruit in a pleasing way on the bed of lettuce and grind a little salt and pepper over it. Dribble the oil over the salad and serve within 30 minutes.

PUDDINGS

During many years of family cooking there have been few occasions when I have been able to get away with providing no pudding. Just as a good meal has a proper beginning so should it end appropriately. If eating alone, I enjoy a small bowl of cherries, fruit from the garden or a home-made truffle with my coffee. But for those like my family and all of my friends who are lovers of pies, puddings and other delicacies I include some favourites.

Some of the recipes can mesh particularly neatly into the rest of one's cooking, for example Chocolate Chinchilla or the Dacquoise utilise a surplus of egg whites in a delicious way. Others are cheap yet delectable—fresh milk quickly becomes junket or, with a little more trouble, a perfect Crême Caramel.

Many cooks concentrate on puddings that are overly rich in cream, sugar and liqueurs. We seem to forget about preparing fruit in an interesting way. Inexpensive pears sautéed quickly in butter, apples wrapped in pastry and baked, rosy rhubarb poached to perfection or a pineapple filled with its own fruit and some sweet grapes with fresh mint. For further fruity inspiration I can't recommend too highly Jane Grigson's *Fruit Book*.

Finally, when planning a meal to include a pudding it is important to remember the balance of the menu. It is usual to start by planning the main course and then deciding which food you wish to serve either side. If, for example, you have already decided upon a soufflé or omelette for pudding, you can then afford to cut down on the protein—meat, fish or cheese—served earlier in the meal. Whether eggs are prepared in a sweet or savoury manner the protein-rich content doesn't change. Poor menu planning leads to the well-known 'impressive-dinner-party' reaction, where the food is over-rich and unnecessarily expensive; everything looks marvellous but the following morning one suffers from a gastronomic hang-over. Unfortunately, too many restaurants in this country also work on this basis. I prefer healthier eating.

225

Cider Jelly with Sabayon Sauce *Serves 4–6*

A lighter, refreshing and very English alternative to a port wine jelly.

300 ml	cold water	½ pint
120 g	granulated sugar	4 oz
1	orange	1
1	lemon	1
1½ tablespoons	powdered gelatine	1½ tablespoons
300 ml, approx	cider	approx ½ pint

Sabayon Sauce:

4	egg yolks	4
90 g	caster sugar	3 oz
90 ml	cider	3 fl oz

Measure the cold water into a measuring jug. Pour almost all of it into a pan and add the sugar and the thinly pared rind of the orange and lemon. Stir over low heat until the sugar is dissolved then simmer the syrup for 4 minutes. Sprinkle the gelatine on to the water remaining in the jug.

Discard the fruit rinds and pour the sugar syrup on to the softened gelatine and stir until clear. Strain the juice from the orange and lemon into the measuring jug and make up to ¾ litre (1¼ pints) with cider.

Pour into a wetted jelly mould and chill until set.

Sabayon Sauce: Whisk the egg yolks and sugar in a bowl set over simmering water until really light and fluffy. Gradually whisk in the cider until you can leave a trail across the sauce. Remove from the heat and continue whisking with the bowl standing in iced water until the mixture is cold.

Dip the mould briefly in hot water and unmould the jelly on to a pretty dish. Pour the Sabayon Sauce around and serve.

Hot Fruit Salad

Serves 4–6

Winter fruits, cooked together, surrender a refreshingly new
flavour compared with serving them cold.

1	eating apple, preferably Cox's orange pippin	1
1	dessert pear, not too ripe	1
1	banana	1
1	seedless tangerine or satsuma	1
	few black or white grapes	
	piece of preserved ginger	
1 tablespoon	ginger syrup	1 tablespoon
	juice of ½ lemon	
1 dessertspoon	clear honey	1 dessertspoon

Peel the apple, pear, banana and tangerine. Dice or thinly
slice the apple and pear into a shallow lidded oven dish, slice
the banana on top and arrange the segments of tangerine
amongst the fruit. Halve the grapes, deseed them (and peel
them, if you wish) and strew over the fruit.

Chop the preserved ginger and mix with the ginger syrup,
lemon juice and honey and pour over the fruit. Cover and
cook in a moderate oven, 190°C, 375°F, Gas Mark 5, for
about 15 minutes or until the fruit is just tender.

Sorbet de St Vaast

Serves 6–8

St Vaast le Hougue is a small Normandy sea-port famous for its oysters. We ate this simple apple sorbet there in a pretty hotel covered by a climbing fuchsia.

¾ kg	really ripe Golden Delicious apples	1½ lb
	rind and juice of ½ lemon	
2–3 tablespoons	water	2–3 tablespoons
120 g	granulated sugar	4 oz
150 ml	water	¼ pint
1	egg white	1
2–3 tablespoons	Calvados	2–3 tablespoons
	langues de chat biscuits or thin shortbread	

Peel, core and quarter the apples. Cook over moderate heat with the thinly pared rind of the lemon and the water until soft.

Remove the lemon rind and reduce the stewed apples to a purée in a blender or processor. Set aside to cool.

Dissolve the sugar in the 150 ml (¼ pint) water and simmer for 5 minutes. Remove from the heat, add the lemon juice and pour on to the purée. Mix well.

Whisk the egg white until stiff and fold into the apple mixture. Turn into a plastic box, cover and freeze. When mushy, whisk again and refreeze.

To serve, scoop the sorbet into pretty glasses and spoon a little Calvados over it. Accompany with biscuits, if you wish.

This sorbet can also be made with Cox's orange pippin but as long as the Golden Delicious are ripe, even shrivelled, they will give a good flavour. They have an undeservedly poor reputation because the British insist on eating them unripe—the name tells all: they should be yellow.

Buttered Pears

By cooking fruit without water you preserve all the flavour; sautéing in butter works well with pears, eating apples or bananas.

4	large, firm, ripe pears	4
60 g	unsalted butter	2 oz
1 tablespoon	caster sugar	1 tablespoon

Peel, core and quarter the pears. Cut into thick slices.

Melt the butter in a pan and when really hot and sizzling add the pears. Sprinkle with sugar and cook over high heat for 6–8 minutes, turning the fruit once. The pears are ready when just starting to colour and the sauce is thick and syrupy.

Serve in hot dishes with pouring cream. If you have it, a splash of Poire William and whipped cream are a worthwhile addition.

Compote of Rhubarb with Orange *Serves 4*

If your mother was a good cook, you probably like rhubarb. If not, prepare to be converted. In my view, cooked with care, rhubarb tastes as exotic and delectable as paw-paw or kiwi. The golden rule is to select slim pink stalks and never let them come into contact with water.

500 g	young rhubarb, without leaves	1 lb
1	sweet orange	1
90–120 g	sugar or honey	3–4 oz

Remove the leaf and stalk ends from the rhubarb. If necessary wipe the stalks clean with a damp cloth. Cut into 2½ cm (1 in) pieces.

In an ovenproof dish or enamelled saucepan, layer the rhubarb with the sugar and the finely grated peel of the orange. Pour the juice of the orange over the mixture and cover.

Cook in a moderate oven, 190°C, 375°F, Gas Mark 5, for 10–15 minutes or on the hob for 7–8 minutes, at any rate long enough to bring to boiling point and then maintain a gentle simmer for 3–4 minutes. Remove from the heat and leave, covered, to complete cooking.

The rhubarb is cooked perfectly if the fruit is tender and the flesh and juice are rosy pink. If the colour has gone the fruit is overcooked.

Variations: add a sliced banana to the fruit when off-heat but still hot or stir some sliced, preserved or crystallised ginger to the fruit when still hot.

Granita Al Caffee

An Italian speciality, a granular water-ice made from sweet black coffee and served, if you wish, topped with whipped cream.

120 g	granulated sugar	4 oz
600 ml	water	1 pint
6 tablespoons	finely ground coffee	6 tablespoons
	a measure of brandy or liqueur (optional)	
4 tablespoons	whipped cream	4 tablespoons
½ teaspoon	finely ground coffee	½ teaspoon

Dissolve the sugar in the water over gentle heat, then simmer the syrup for 3 minutes. Remove from the heat, add the coffee and stir. Leave, uncovered, for 10 minutes for the flavour to be extracted.

Strain the coffee through a filter paper and let it cool. Pour into an ice tray or plastic box. Cover and freeze, stirring from time to time, until mushy and granular.

Spoon the granita into 4 stemmed glasses. If you wish, run a little brandy or liqueur over the ice and spoon whipped cream on top. Sprinkle with the rest of the ground coffee.

Clyst William Apple Dumplings   *Serves 4*

Samuel Coleridge, who was born at Ottery St Mary, just five miles away, was reputed to have said that 'a man cannot have a pure mind who refuses apple-dumplings'. Here is my Devon version, since quinces seem to grow as effortlessly as apples in our village.

Shortcrust pastry:

250 g	plain flour	8 oz
120 g	butter	4 oz
30 g	caster sugar	1 oz
4 tablespoons	milk	4 tablespoons
4	large eating apples, Ellison's orange or Cox's orange pippin	4
	knob of butter	
4	slices cooked quince *or* quince jelly	4
	egg yolk, for glazing	

Make the shortcrust pastry with the flour, butter, sugar and milk and chill it, wrapped, for 30 minutes.

Peel and core the apples. Slip a little butter into the bottom of each and then fit a quince slice in each apple (with a runcible spoon, of course) or fill with jelly instead.

Divide the pastry into 4 pieces. Roll each piece into a circle large enough to enclose the apple. Cut off any surplus and squeeze the joins together well. Turn the dumpling over and place it smooth side up on a buttered baking sheet.

Make a good-sized round steam vent on top and surround it with 3 or 4 pastry leaves cut from the trimmings.

Brush the dumplings with egg yolk and bake in a hot oven, 200°C, 400°F, Gas Mark 6, for 30–45 minutes until the apple is cooked. Lower the heat if the pastry browns too quickly. Serve with cream.

Minted Pineapple Surprise

Serves 6–8

In mid-summer pineapples are often delightfully cheap on market stalls and, if fully ripe and tender to the touch, need to be eaten straight away.

1	ripe pineapple	1
	caster sugar to taste	
½ kg	seedless grapes	1 lb
12	mint leaves, chopped	12

Cut a lid from the pineapple, keeping the plume intact. Using a vegetable knife and a sharp spoon, remove the flesh from the centre of the pineapple and scrape the walls smooth. Store the pineapple shell and lid in a cool place until needed. Select the tender fruit for the compote and cook the core and any harder flesh with some sugar to make a syrup for using in fruit salad (store it in the freezer).

Roughly chop the selected pineapple into a bowl and sprinkle with caster sugar. Add the washed grapes (I don't peel seedless grapes since their skin is thin) and the chopped mint. Cover and chill the mixture for 1–2 hours.

Spoon the fruit compote back into the pineapple shell and replace the lid. Serve with any surplus juice in a separate jug or whisk it into some whipped cream.

Variation: try other combinations of good value summer fruits with the pineapple, such as peaches and strawberries.

Iced Mocha Soufflé

Serves 8

I devised this recipe to capture the irresistible combination of chocolate with coffee which gives the flavour known as mocha, named after the Yemeni city of Moka. Such a rich concoction is best served in small glasses and any that is over can be stored in the freezer for another time.

4 tablespoons	ground coffee	4 tablespoons
150 ml	creamy milk	¼ pint
2	egg whites	2
120 g	caster sugar	4 oz
120 g	plain chocolate	4 oz
150 ml	double cream	¼ pint

Measure the coffee into a small glass or enamel saucepan. Add the milk and heat slowly until boiling point. Immediately remove from the heat and set aside to infuse.

Set a good-sized bowl over simmering water. Add the egg whites and sugar and whisk (preferably with a hand-held electric beater) for about 5 minutes until the mixture is cooked to a fairly firm foam. Remove the bowl and replace it with a small bowl containing the chocolate broken into pieces.

Continue to whisk the egg whites off the heat for 3 minutes.

Strain the coffee on to the melted chocolate and stir to combine, then stir until cool.

Whip the cream until stiff but still glossy. Gradually whisk in the coffee/chocolate mixture and fold into the cooked meringue.

Turn the mixture into a bowl or plastic box. Cover and freeze for 4–6 hours until firm. Serve straight from the freezer in small scoopfuls.

Crème Caramel

Serves 4–6

A French classic, low in cost but very high on taste and well worth taking the trouble to perfect.

100 g	granulated sugar	3½ oz
75 ml	water	3 fl oz
600 ml	milk	1 pint
2 tablespoons	vanilla sugar	2 tablespoons
	vanilla pod	
2	eggs	2
2	egg yolks	2

In a small heavy based saucepan dissolve the sugar in the water over gentle heat. Raise the heat and boil the syrup until it turns a dark golden-brown. Remove from heat, let the bubbles subside and pour into a warmed ¾ litre (1¼ pint) soufflé dish or straight sided oven dish. Tilt the dish to coat the bottom and sides and stand it in a bain-marie or roasting tin half-full of warm water.

Heat the milk with the vanilla sugar and/or pod. In a bowl, beat the eggs and egg yolks with a fork. Remove the vanilla pod and pour the hot milk on to the eggs, stir, then strain into the caramelled dish.

Bake, covered with a piece of foil, in a moderate oven, 180°C, 350°F, Gas Mark 4, for about 45 minutes or until set. Allow to cool in the bain-marie, then transfer to the refrigerator—it will keep, covered, for 2 days.

Just before serving carefully turn out the Crème Caramel on to a perfectly flat plate with a rim to contain the syrup.

Peaches in Red Wine

Serves 4

We usually think of pouring sweet white wine or liqueur over fresh peaches but the Italians use red wine with fruit to great effect.

4	large ripe peaches	4
150 ml	cheap red wine, preferably Italian	¼ pint
1 tablespoon	demerara sugar	1 tablespoon
½	stick cinnamon	½

Cover the peaches with boiling water for 10 seconds. Replace the hot water with cold. Peel the peaches and slice them into a shallow bowl.

Heat the wine with the sugar and the cinnamon stick until the sugar has dissolved and the wine is very hot.

Remove the cinnamon stick and pour the wine over the peaches. Leave for at least 30 minutes. Serve warm or chilled.

Lapsang Souchong Tea Cream   *Serves 6*

A tea cream is a nineteenth-century notion; made with Lapsang Souchong or gunpowder tea it is entrancing. When served by candlelight on a winter evening the unmoulded cream looks like alabaster.

2 tablespoons	Lapsang Souchong tea	2 tablespoons
4 tablespoons	boiling water	4 tablespoons
3 tablespoons	caster sugar	3 tablespoons
500 ml	single cream	¾ pint
4 teaspoons	powdered gelatine	4 teaspoons
2 tablespoons	cold water	2 tablespoons
	a little mild tasting salad oil	

Measure the tea into a saucepan and pour over the boiling water. Add the caster sugar and cream.

Slowly bring contents of the pan to the boil over gentle heat, stirring all the time. Taste every so often until the cream is well flavoured. Remove from the heat and strain the cream into a bowl to cool.

Soften the gelatine in the cold water, then heat gently until dissolved. Cool a little then pour in a thin stream into the tea flavoured cream, stirring all the time.

Pour into a lightly oiled mould or into individual glass dishes. Chill until set, then dip the mould briefly into very hot water. Invert and unmould the cream on to a serving plate.

Serve with thin shortbread or almond biscuits.

Chocolate Chinchilla

A good way of using surplus egg whites, from Elizabeth David's *Salts, Spices and Aromatics in the English Kitchen*.

6	egg whites	6
90 g	caster sugar	3 oz
60 g	cocoa powder	2 oz
2–3 teaspoons	ground cinnamon	2–3 teaspoons
	pouring cream	
	a little sherry, rum or brandy	

Whisk the egg whites until stiff. Whisk in one tablespoon of sugar. Sieve the rest of the sugar with the cocoa and cinnamon and fold into the egg white.

Turn into a buttered 1 litre (1¾ pint) ring mould, preferably with a straight central funnel.

Cook in a bain-marie in the centre of a slow oven, 160°C, 325°F, Gas Mark 3, for about 45 minutes.

Remove from the oven carefully and leave to cool in the tin. It will shrink somewhat while cooling but the chinchilla is then easily turned out on to a serving plate. Serve with pouring cream flavoured with sherry, rum or brandy.

Tarte au Citron

Serves 8–10

A superb French Sunday tart. True budget gourmets make this for a fraction of the price of those in a Soho patisserie.

Pâte sucrée:

150 g	plain flour	5 oz
75 g	caster sugar (vanilla flavoured)	2½ oz
90 g	unsalted butter, at room temperature	3 oz
2	egg yolks	2

Tranches de citron confites:

2	medium sized lemons	2
½ litre	water	¾ pint
250 g	granulated sugar	8 oz
1	vanilla pod	1

Crème d'amandes:

2	eggs	2
120 g	caster sugar	4 oz
120 g	ground almonds	4 oz
	grated rind of ½ lemon	
15 g	crystallised angelica	½ oz

Sieve the flour and sugar on to a marble surface or into the base of a cool wide bowl. Make a well in the centre and add the butter and egg yolks. Using the fingertips only, mix the butter and egg yolks gradually, drawing in a little flour all the time as you do so. When the mixture starts to cohere in a mass, make a ball of the dough and leave on a plate under an upturned bowl to rest. Chill if the pastry is very soft.

Wash the lemons and cut into very thin slices, discarding the pips. Cook in a glass or enamel saucepan with the water over moderate heat, until the lemon peel is clear and breaks easily (as for marmalade), about 30–40 minutes.

Now add the sugar and vanilla pod and stir gently now and again until the sugar is dissolved. Then boil steadily for 15–20 minutes. Lift out the lemon slices and vanilla pod with a slotted spoon and reduce the liquid over high heat to about 150 ml (¼ pint). This syrup should now set when cool.

On a floured board roll out the pâte sucrée to line a buttered 23 cm (9 in) metal flan tin with a removable base. There should be no pastry over.

Make the crème d'amandes by beating the eggs with the sugar and then adding the ground almonds and lemon rind. Spoon into the pastry case, smoothing it level.

Bake on a preheated baking sheet in a moderately hot oven, 200°C, 400°F, Gas Mark 6, for 20–25 minutes, until the pastry is golden and the filling is cooked.

Brush the filling with warm liquid syrup. Arrange the lemon slices (some may need to be curved round to fit) attractively over the filling. Cut diamonds from the angelica and place them evenly between the lemon slices. Pour the rest of the syrup evenly over the filling and put aside to set. Serve cold.

Almond and Tangerine Dacquoise

Serves 12

A good party cake that can be made ahead and frozen. Cut when half frozen.

6	egg whites	6
350 g	caster sugar	12 oz
120 g	ground almonds	4 oz
1 teaspoon	finely grated tangerine rind	1 teaspoon
30 g	flaked almonds, toasted	1 oz
6	tangerines	6
	juice of 1 small lemon	
60 g	caster sugar	2 oz
2	eggs	2
300 ml	double cream	½ pint
1 teaspoon	icing sugar	1 teaspoon

Draw two circles 20 cm (8 in) across on two sheets of Bakewell vegetable parchment. Fix each sheet to a baking tray with a smear of butter at each corner.

Whisk the egg whites until stiff. Gradually whisk in half the sugar. Now mix the rest of the sugar with the ground almonds and the grated tangerine rind and carefully fold into the meringue. Spread the mixture to cover the two circles and sprinkle the top of each with the toasted almonds.

Bake in a cool oven, 100°C, 200°F, Gas Mark ½, for 2 hours. Allow to cool in the oven.

Finely grate the rinds of two tangerines into a bowl and add the juice from all the tangerines and the lemon. Stir in the caster sugar and eggs and whisk gently over simmering water until thickened. This takes about 10–15 minutes. Remove from the heat and cool the tangerine curd by standing the bowl in cold water.

Whip the cream until thick. Gradually fold in the tangerine curd. Place one meringue round on a flat pretty dish, spread the tangerine cream on top and cover with the other meringue round.

Dust the top of the dacquoise with sieved icing sugar and chill for two hours before serving, or freeze.

Compote of Clementines with Cointreau

Serves 4

Citrus fruit, cooked whole, reveals a fresh flavour. Clementines, seedless satsumas or tangerines all taste wonderful this way.

120 g	sugar, granulated	4 oz
300 ml	water	½ pint
	strip of clementine peel	
16–20	clementines	16–20
2 tablespoons	Cointreau	2 tablespoons

Dissolve the sugar in the water over low heat. Add the strip of peel and bring to the boil. Simmer the syrup for 3–4 minutes, then discard the peel.

Peel the clementines carefully (keep the peel for drying) making sure not to puncture the flesh. Poach the fruit in the syrup for 4–5 minutes, turning over the fruit once. Do not overcook or they will lose their fresh flavour and will shrivel.

Use a slotted spoon to remove the fruit to a pretty shallow dish. Add the Cointreau to the syrup and pour over the clementines. Serve warm or cold.

Banana and Blackberry Cobbler

Serves 4–6

The cobbler is an excellent American idea for a hot pudding.
Quicker to make than pastry, the scone-like crust makes a
good contrast to the dark fruity base.

500 g	blackberries	1 lb
120 g	sugar, granulated	4 oz
2	large bananas	2
1 tablespoon	cornflour	1 tablespoon

Cobbler:

250 g	self-raising flour	8 oz
½ teaspoon	baking powder	½ teaspoon
60 g	vanilla sugar	2 oz
60 g	butter or soft margarine	2 oz
to make 150 ml	an egg mixed with milk	to make ¼ pint
	pouring cream, to serve	

Cook the blackberries in a pan with the sugar over low heat
until the juice begins to run. Add the bananas cut in thick
slices. Mix the cornflour with a tablespoon of cold water and
pour into the hot fruit.

Spoon the mixture into a heatproof dish deep enough to
be only half full.

Sieve the flour and baking powder into a bowl. Stir in the
sugar and add the butter cut into small pieces. Pour in the
liquid and use a knife to mix to a soft dough.

Place about 12 dessertspoonfuls of the mixture on the fruit,
so that the surface is covered.

Bake in a hot oven, 220°C, 425°F, Gas Mark 7, for 30
minutes, until the cobbler is crisp and golden. Serve with
pouring cream.

Egg Noodles with Poppy Seeds and Honey

Serves 4

The versatile noodle makes an appearance for pudding—exceedingly popular with children, I find.

Noodle dough:

120 g	plain flour	4 oz
	pinch salt	
2	egg yolks	2
2 tablespoons	cold water	2 tablespoons
45 g	unsalted butter	1½ oz
4 tablespoons	blue poppy seeds	4 tablespoons
2 tablespoons	clear honey	2 tablespoons
	grated rind of ½ lemon	
	pouring cream (optional)	

Sieve the flour and salt into a bowl. Mix the egg yolks with the water and gradually mix into the flour. Or turn all the ingredients into a processor and mix to a soft dough.

Roll out the dough as explained for home-made pasta (see p. 82) and leave to dry for 30 minutes. Roll up and cut into ½ cm (¼ in) wide slices. Allow to dry and then cook in boiling salted water until *al dente*.

Meanwhile melt the butter in a pan and stir in the poppy seeds and honey. Gently cook together for 2 minutes. Add the drained noodles and lemon rind. Toss together over low heat for 2 minutes and serve with a little cream poured over if you wish.

Coffee Junket with Chocolate   *Serves 4*

One summer I experimented endlessly with different junkets.
This was one of the most popular.

600 ml	fresh milk	1 pint
1 tablespoon	caster sugar	1 tablespoon
75 g	plain chocolate	2½ oz
3–4 teaspoons	liquid coffee essence	3–4 teaspoons
2 teaspoons	Stone's Essence of Rennet	2 teaspoons

Warm the milk with the sugar, stirring until dissolved, to blood
heat (37°C, 98°F).

Break the chocolate into pieces and melt in a small bowl
over hot water.

Remove the milk from the heat and stir in the coffee
essence and the rennet.

Pour into four small dishes for serving.

Trickle the melted chocolate into the junket, making a
swirling pattern. Some will sink, some will stay on top.

Leave the junket to set at room temperature. This normally
takes about 20–40 minutes.

Rum Omelette Soufflé

What a transformation in an omelette if you separate the eggs
and add air! Simple and excellent.

3	eggs	3
30 g	caster sugar	1 oz
2 tablespoons	dark Jamaican rum	2 tablespoons
1 teaspoon	plain flour	1 teaspoon
	small knob of butter	
	a little caster sugar	

Separate the eggs into two bowls. Beat the sugar, half the rum
and the flour into the yolks.

Whisk the egg whites until stiff. Fold into the yolk mixture.

Set the grill on high.

Melt the butter in 20 cm (8 in) omelette pan. When it foams
pour in the omelette mixture. Cook over moderate heat for
2–3 minutes.

Then move under the preheated grill to complete the
cooking until the top is beginning to brown.

Sprinkle with caster sugar, return to the grill and allow to
caramelise a little. Warm the remaining rum and set alight if
you wish. Anyhow, lighted or not, pour the warmed rum over
the omelette soufflé and serve straight away.

Alternatively the omelette can be cooked in the oven. Pour
the mixture into a hot buttered oven dish and bake in a hot
oven, 200°C, 400°F, Gas Mark 6, for 10–12 minutes. Cut
into wedges to serve.

Chocolate Orange Truffles   *Makes about 18*

To end a gourmet's meal with a flourish, serve with coffee.

150 g	plain dessert chocolate	5 oz
1 teaspoon	finely grated orange rind *or* powdered dried orange peel	1 teaspoon
150 ml	double cream	¼ pint
2 tablespoons	Cointreau or Grand Marnier	2 tablespoons
60 g	ground almonds	2 oz
60 g	plain chocolate, grated into curls	2 oz

Break the chocolate into pieces and melt in a bowl over hot water. Stir in the orange rind and cool a little.

Whisk the cream with the Cointreau until stiff and fold into the cooled, but still liquid, chocolate with the ground almonds.

Chill the mixture in the refrigerator until firm.

Take teaspoons of the mixture, shape into a ball and roll in the grated chocolate. Arrange the truffles (in brown or gold paper cases, if you wish) in a pretty dish and keep chilled until ready to serve.

INDEX